*From the Pen of
a She-Rebel*

WOMEN'S DIARIES AND LETTERS OF THE SOUTH
Carol Bleser, Series Editor

From the Pen of a She-Rebel

THE CIVIL WAR DIARY OF EMILIE RILEY McKINLEY

Edited by Gordon A. Cotton

UNIVERSITY OF SOUTH CAROLINA PRESS

UNIVERSITY OF SOUTH CAROLINA **BICENTENNIAL**

Published in Columbia, South Carolina, by the
University of South Carolina Press

Manufactured in the United States of America

05   04   03   02   01   5   4   3   2   1

Library of Congress Cataloging-in-Publication Data

McKinley, Emilie Riley.
  From the pen of a she-rebel : the Civil War diary of Emilie Riley McKinley /
edited by Gordon A. Cotton.
    p.   cm. — (Womens diaries and letters of the South)
  Includes bibliographical references and index.
  ISBN 1-57003-356-0 (cloth : alk. paper)
  1. McKinley, Emilie Riley—Diaries. 2. United States—History—Civil War,
1861–1865—Personal narratives, Confederate. 3. Vicksburg (Miss.)—
History—Civil War, 1861–1865—Personal narratives. 4. Women—
Mississippi—Vicksburg Region—Diaries. 5. Vicksburg Region (Miss.)—
Biography. I. Cotton, Gordon A., 1936– II. Title. III. Women's diaries and
letters of the nineteenth-century South
  E605 .M14   2001
  973.7'82—dc21   00-012671

For Dr. Martha M. Bigelow,
who made the study and learning
of history a pleasure

CONTENTS

ILLUSTRATIONS

SERIES EDITOR'S PREFACE

From the Pen of a She-Rebel: The Civil War Diary of Emilie Riley McKinley is the thirteenth volume in what had been the Women's Diaries and Letters of the Nineteenth-Century South series. This series has been redefined and is now titled Women's Diaries and Letters of the South, enabling us to include some remarkably fine works from the twentieth century. This series includes a number of never-before-published diaries, some collections of unpublished correspondence, and a few reprints of published diaries—a potpourri of nineteenth-century and, now, twentieth-century Southern women's writings.

The series enables women to speak for themselves, providing readers with a rarely opened window into Southern society before, during, and after the American Civil War and into the twentieth century. The significance of these letters and journals lies not only in the personal revelations and the writing talent of these women authors but also in the range and versatility of the documents' contents. Taken together, these publications will tell us much about the heyday and the fall of the Cotton Kingdom, the mature years of the "peculiar institution," the war years, the adjustment of the South to a new social order following the defeat of the Confederacy, and the New South of the twentieth century. Through these writings, the reader will also be presented with firsthand accounts of everyday life and social events, courtships and marriages, family life and travels, religion and education, and the life-and-death matters that made up the ordinary and extraordinary world of the American South.

From the Pen of a She-Rebel, edited by Gordon A. Cotton, is a diary that spans the ten months from May 1863 to March 1864 covering the siege, the surrender, and much of the occupation of Vicksburg. It is a lively, incisive work, written by someone who fully appreciated the significance of the events she was experiencing and who strove to make her diary a worthy record of those events. Her forceful personality as someone who never accepted defeat and occupation dominates the text. McKinley's story is a strong counterexample to those who argue that the deep discontent of

Southern white women contributed to the Confederacy's defeat. This is a work of local history, important for the information it contains, but it transcends its genre by its liveliness and the force of the writer's personality.

CAROL BLESER

PREFACE

Her opinions and observations were the most Southern in sentiment, and there was no question of her allegiance to the Confederate cause, so the last thing one would expect while reading the Civil War diary of Emilie McKinley was that she was a Yankee.

McKinley, who taught the children of several planter families in the Mount Alban community east of Vicksburg, Miss., during the early 1860s, began keeping a diary on 18 May 1863 and wrote daily at first, then less frequently for the next ten months, concluding her entries on 18 March 1864.

She made no effort to hide the fact of her nativity, nor did she blatantly reveal it; after all, hers was a private journal, not intended for publication or for others to see. The first hint in her writing that she was not a Southerner by birth was made on 21 May 1863, her fourth entry in the diary, when she wrote that her feelings about the North were "unnatural" and then asked herself if she could ever visit above the Mason-Dixon line again. Her answer was an emphatic no! In another entry she told a Yankee soldier that she was a Northern woman who agreed with the South.

Emilie Riley McKinley was born in Pennsylvania, one of ten children in the household of John McKinley, a West Chester merchant. He was described by a grandson as "a man of large ideas but little success" who "gave all his children fine educations."[1] Emilie became a teacher, but, other than her sojourn in Mississippi, the only place of residence of which she wrote was Tennessee.

In her diary McKinley made a few references to family, mentioning one time that she had received word that her sister, whom she called "Sis," had died, as had someone named Joe. She never mentioned any others, including a brother named Tom who was in the Union army and commanded United States Colored Troops. Perhaps she did not know it; if she did she certainly would not have approved. Tom McKinley was wounded at Chapin's Farm, Va., and died in the hospital at Fortress Monroe in 1864.[2] McKinley's sister Adelaide married Dr. David Elmore Bostwick, a physician from Connecticut. Their son, Dr. Arthur E. Bostwick, was librarian for the St. Louis Public Library from 1909 to 1938. He had possession of McKinley's diary until his death in 1942, and in 1961 his daughter-in-law, Mrs. A. Linn

Bostwick, gave it and other papers and items that had belonged to Bostwick to the Missouri Historical Society in St. Louis. It had been almost a century since the diary had been written.

I first became acquainted with the diary several years ago when Tom Brooks, a senior volunteer with the Missouri Historical Society, called the Old Court House Museum in Vicksburg, Miss., where I am the director, and asked questions about some of the individuals mentioned by McKinley. I was familiar with many of them, as they were of pioneer Warren County families. After exchanging letters with Brooks and securing a copy of the diary, I plunged into the task of reading, which sometimes meant deciphering, and making notes about people, places, and events contained in its pages.

One of the most elusive characters in the diary was the diarist. Gleaned from her entries were tidbits that she was an Episcopalian and that she played chess well enough to beat a Missouri officer several times. No photographs of her have been discovered. Even her age is a mystery, though she was young enough for teenage girls to be comfortable in her company but old enough to command their respect. She was also perfectly at ease around older women. McKinley left Vicksburg and Warren County probably in 1864 with no hint of her destination but an indication that she would continue teaching.

McKinley wrote well, and it appears that the diary was neither revised nor corrected later, other than that all entries before 9 June 1863 were written in pencil and then gone over with ink. The letters and words seem to match, though she erased two lines for the 21 May 1863 entry and wrote over them. Perhaps she was rephrasing, but the two original lines are missing. The only other portion of the diary that is missing is a copy of a letter that Mrs. Batchelor, in whose home McKinley lived, wrote to General Grant. The letter was copied on 23 May 1863, but it was cut out of the diary just after a sentence in which Mrs. Batchelor said "I have to tell you an act, that will make any gentleman *blush*. . . . " Of course, part of the entry on the back of the page was also destroyed.

Other than an occasional word added for clarity and enclosed in bracket to distinguish it from the original, the diary has been left in the words of McKinley. Changes in format have been made, as I have paragraphed the diary and divided it into chapters. The dialogue ran together in lines, and I have restructured it for easier reading. There has also been occasional modification of punctuation and capitalization.

McKinley began each entry with the date in abbreviated form; the dates have been broadened to include not only the day but also the month, date, and year. While the diarist often used initials to refer to individuals, most of those entries have been expanded to the use of the surname. For example, "Mrs. B" has been changed to "Mrs. Batchelor." Only twice were surnames misspelled—Boles instead of Bolls and Bryan instead of Brien; I have corrected both. Notes have been included to provide background and details about people, places and events.

I have often relied on my fellow employee at the Old Court House Museum, Jeff T. Giambrone, in helping interpret passages difficult to read and in sharing his extensive knowledge of the Vicksburg campaign; his assistance is greatly appreciated. I am indebted to Mrs. Martha Clevenger, former archivist of the Missouri Historical Society, for providing a copy of the diary and also securing permission for editing and publishing. I also appreciate the encouragement and assistance of Chuck Hill, present archivist for the society, in completing this project.

I thank Angie Noland and Earl Batchelor for clarifying Noland/Batchelor family genealogies; Hobbs Freeman and Mary Lois Ragland for technical and clerical assistance; Nelma Crutcher for help in research; and Dr. Christopher Waldrep of the University of Eastern Illinois for his encouragement and suggestions. I thank Catherine Fry and Alex Moore of the University of South Carolina Press for their interest, encouragement, and belief in this project. Without the interest of Bob Dyer, historian/folklorist/musician from Boonville, Mo., who undertook a records search, much of the provenance of the diary would have remained a mystery. To Tom Brooks I will always be grateful, for without his curiosity to know more the diary would still be filed in the Missouri Historical Society archives.

From the Pen of
a She-Rebel

PROLOGUE

"Madam, I am ashamed to tell you we have been terribly whipped,"[1] a Confederate cavalryman told Margaret Lord, who stood on the porch of a home only two miles from the Big Black River. Ironically, Mrs. Lord and her family had fled Vicksburg, hoping to find a place of safety in the country.

Cannons still boomed at the scene of battle, and shells shrieked through the air as tired and dusty soldiers, many frightened, all disheartened, began the rush toward Vicksburg, some twelve miles to the west. At first there were only a few; they were joined by fleeing families hoping to escape the Union army. Soon the roads were clogged with soldiers and civilians and ambulance wagons carrying the dead and wounded.

The day was Sunday, 17 May 1863. Only a month earlier, Adm. David D. Porter's federal fleet had successfully passed Vicksburg in the middle of the night, and though the Confederates had lighted the sky with giant bonfires along the city's waterfront, and buildings had been set afire on the Louisiana shore to illuminate the river, the Southern guns were able to inflict but little damage.

Gen. U.S. Grant's army moved down the west bank and, like a swarm of locusts, left a path of destruction. Determined Missouri and Louisiana Rebels, manning some big guns at the confluence of the Big Black with the Mississippi River, denied the Yankees a landing at Grand Gulf, so the Northern troops continued their march through the Louisiana countryside to Hardtimes where their ships ferried them across to the town of Bruinsburg on the Mississippi shore.

Several miles inland, Confederates led by Gen. John S. Bowen met the Yankees at the Schaffer plantation. Inferior only in numbers, Bowen's boys were unable to repulse those in blue. The Confederates fell back to Port Gibson, and then across Bayou Pierre.

Grant was on his way to Vicksburg, but his was not the first attempt to take the city. In the spring of 1862, Adm. David G. Farragut's fleet had come up the Mississippi as far as Vicksburg, leaving behind a string of white flags as New Orleans, Baton Rouge, and Natchez fell along with other river towns, some after fierce fighting, others without a battle. Farragut's shelling of Vicksburg only strengthened the determination of the Confederates to hold their fortress on the bluffs, and a defiant commander informed the Yankee admiral that "Mississippians don't know, and refuse to learn, how to surrender to an enemy. If Commander Farragut or Brigadier-General Butler can teach them, let them come and try."[2]

As the waters of the Mississippi began to fall, and the courage of the Southerners remained unshaken, the Northern ships steamed back toward the Gulf of Mexico. The capture of Vicksburg would require another tact at another time.

Again an effort was made at Christmas in 1862, just a few miles north of the city, when Gen. William T. Sherman attempted a landing beneath the bluffs along Chickasaw Bayou only to be met by eight thousand Confederates manning the lofty fortifications. Sherman, with four times as many men, was no match for them. Pushing his men through the icy swamp waters at the base of the hills, he lost over seventeen hundred to the South's 207—and learned that war really was hell.

Sherman's partner, Grant, had been unable to join him, for Confederates under Gen. Earl Van Dorn had raided his supply depot in north Mississippi, destroying over one million dollars worth of war materials and temporarily crippling Grant's efforts. Other ideas were thrashed about. Perhaps Vicksburg could be reached through the bayous in the flat delta lands north of the city, but attempts to penetrate the interior with small tinclads found them often hemmed in by Confederates felling trees in the streams, impeding progress and threatening escape. The final plan, bolder but also risky, would be to invade the state from the river somewhere south of Vicksburg, cut a path northeast toward the capital, Jackson, and then turn due west toward Vicksburg's back door. The plan, hazy at best, began to materialize when the men came ashore at Bruinsburg.

From Port Gibson the Yankees struck out through the countryside, forsaking their supplies, living off the larders of the plantations along the way, leaving behind hungry women and children and slaves. There were skirmishes at Willows, Hankinson's Ferry, Rocky Springs, and Fourteen Mile Creek, and there were battles at Raymond and Champion's Hill. Confederates commanded by Gen. Joseph E. Johnston put up brief resistance before abandoning the capital, which the Yankees burned, then about-faced and marched toward Vicksburg, fifty miles away.

Confederates, under the command of Gen. John C. Pemberton, fought and delayed, but they were hardly a match for the Yankees who pillaged their way through Clinton and Bolton and Brownsville before the armies met for a showdown on the farm of Sid and Matilda Champion a few miles from Edwards' Station. On the gently rolling hills the Southerners came close to turning the tide, but they were outnumbered and outgeneraled. Grant's men carried the day, and the Confederates began their retreat toward the Big Black River several miles distant. Only a month earlier, the Yankees had run the river batteries at Vicksburg.

Earlier in the campaign, in planning defenses, the Confederates had constructed a series of rifle pits and cotton-bale breastworks across a neck of land on the east bank of the Big Black River, hoping to slow the advance of the enemy. Pemberton's men had filled an adjacent bayou with brush and trees; in front was an open field that the enemy would have to cross. It was a strong position, and Pemberton hoped to hold it until Gen. W. W. Loring's forces, who had become separated from the main army, could rejoin him. As Pemberton marched toward Vicksburg, he left three bridges and eighteen guns to await Loring, who never came. In the one-hour "holding action," ten thousand Yankees routed four thousand Rebels, capturing over seventeen hundred of them along with the guns. The defeated Confederates slowed Grant's army only by burning bridges that spanned the small, muddy river. By the next day the blue mass was crossing on its own pontoon bridges.

The rank-and-file Confederates, all retreating, some dropping their guns and running, were not the only members of their army dismayed by the turn of events. Riding from the Big Black toward the rural hamlet of Bovina, Pemberton told a staff officer, "Just 30 years ago I began my cadetship at the U.S. Military Academy. Today, the same date, that career is ended in disaster and disgrace."[3]

Earlier in the day Mary Loughborough, who had followed her Missouri soldier husband to the beleaguered city, attended services at the Methodist church and heard a message of cheer and comfort. Despite the beauty and seeming tranquility of the day, however, she wrote in her diary that "an anxious gloom hung over the faces of men"[4] and all seemed to be waiting for the news of some disaster.

When it came, Emma Balfour watched as the defeated men streamed into the city, and she wrote she hoped "never to witness again such a scene as the return of our routed army." It was a painful duty for her to record what had happened, but she nevertheless wrote, "We are defeated—our army in confusion and the carnage—awful, awful!" The streets were crowded with wagons, men, cannons, and horses, and "nothing like order prevailed."[5]

The heart of the city went out to the weary soldiers, and residents shared all they had with them. Emma Balfour put food on her spacious back gallery, and neighbors brought water. On Farmer Street, Elizabeth Eggleston and her daughter Mahala Roach kept food and water on the porch for the passing Confederates. Even Dora Miller, a pro-Union resident who had recently moved to the city, wrote sympathetically, "I shall never forget that woeful sight of a beaten, demoralized army that came rushing back—humanity in the last throes of endurance. Wan, hollow-eyed, ragged, footsore, bloody—the men limped along, unarmed but followed by siege guns, ambulances, gun-carriages, and wagons in aimless confusion. At twilight two or three bands on the courthouse hill and other points began playing 'Dixie,' 'Bonnie Blue Flag,' and so on; and drums began to beat all about. I suppose they were rallying the scattered army."[6]

By evening the next day the Confederates had moved to their positions protecting the city. Grant's army had crossed the Big Black, and the siege of Vicksburg was about to begin.

Many city residents had fled to the country seeking refuge, and some planters had taken slaves and valuables and sought sanctuary in the interiors of Alabama or Texas. Those who stayed behind became virtual prisoners of war, subjected to constant bombardment and shelling with no chance to escape if inside the city, or if living outside of town, threatened daily by marauding stragglers and often by regular soldiers from Grant's army.

Ellen Batchelor and her younger children were among those to remain; her sons were in the Confederate army. The plantation, Hoboken, was about seven miles east of Vicksburg near the Mount Alban community and only a few miles south of the main route taken by the armies. A widow of forty-two, Mrs. Batchelor had run the plantation since the death of her husband, Napoleon B. Batchelor, in the fall of 1850. They had married in 1837 in Jefferson County, where her ancestors, the Nolands, were among the earliest settlers. The Batchelors, French Huguenots, had come to the Mississippi Territory from South Carolina, and Napoleon's father, Thomas, was among those who helped shape the new state's constitution in 1817. Ellen was the second of eight children born to Pearce and Elizabeth Galtney Noland. Of her six brothers, one married Emily Dent, a relative of Julia Grant, and another married Victoria Morancy, whose grandfather was an adopted child of Charles Carroll of Carrollton, last surviving signer of the Declaration of Independence.

When Napoleon B. Batchelor died, he left his wife with not only a plantation to operate, but also five children to raise. On the eve of the Civil War, Thomas, twenty-two, was a medical student and George, twenty, was studying law. The other children were Victoria, fifteen; Ellen, thirteen; and Eugenia, ten. Victoria had attended a girl's school in New Jersey.

Ellen Noland Batchelor's parents owned Sligo, a nearby plantation on the Big Black, which their youngest son, Hal Noland, operated after their deaths just before the war. Two other brothers, Thomas Vaughn Noland and Pearce Noland, Jr., lived nearby, and brother Joseph Noland lived across the Mississippi River in Madison Parish, La.

Eighty-five slaves were used to operate Hoboken. Cotton was the cash crop, but corn was also raised for both human and animal consumption, and gardens and orchards supplied most of the food needed. Mrs. Batchelor also had a herd of milch cows. Her home was a comfortable two-story frame house, and she paid luxury taxes on a piano, a clock, and a carriage. Nearby were the usual farm buildings, such as a gin house, blacksmith shop, barns, sheds, and the slave quarters.

Mrs. Batchelor and some of her slaves were communicants of St. Alban's Episcopal Church, several miles northeast toward Bovina. Near the Batchelor home was a Baptist church and also a Methodist, both named Mount Alban and each with a cemetery, though the Nolands and Batchelors buried their dead in the family graveyard at Sligo.

There was also a Masonic lodge at Mount Alban and a small private school which children of several families in the vicinity, including the Batchelors, attended. Emilie McKinley had been the instructor since about the time the war began. Though she lived mostly at the Batchelor home, she also stayed with other families in the Mount Alban community.

On 18 May 1863, the day after the battle of the Big Black River, McKinley expressed her anguish at the Confederate defeat on the pages of a journal. For the next ten months she wrote of heartaches and tragedy, of humor and irony, of daring and personal heroism and acts of kindness, and of the social upheaval that engulfed the Mount Alban community and the Batchelor family in particular.

Emilie R. McKinley
May 1863
Miss Emilie Riley McKinley
alias

"De gustibus non disputandum."
—Cicero

Concerning taste (it must) not be argued,
or
There is no accounting for taste.

1

"My Blood Boils
As I Write"

Yesterday was one of the saddest days it has ever been my fate to have experienced; our troops retreated from Big Black bridge to Vicksburg. They could have held it but were afraid of being flanked as they would have been – Oh! my heart ached, as I hope it never will again.

Mrs. Batchelor had her cattle, sheep, etc., driven to town early in the morning. Dr. Batchelor went to Vicksburg about 2 o'clock, carrying the carriage horses, May [and] Bob, also provisions to last himself. This morning Mrs. Batchelor regretted having sent her carriage horses and said, "Tom had been after me to send those horses away. I believe I could have hid them." She almost thought she would send for them but was rather doubtful about them being sent back.

Well, about 3 o'clock this evening a man rode up to the door. Mrs. Noland[1] ran out and said, "Any news, Sir?"

"None," was the answer.

"Are you going to Vicksburg?"

"Yes, if I can get there."

"Are there any Yankees about?"

"Plenty," he said, "for I am a Northern soldier. Not a Yankee though."

There was an expressive silence of a minute. The Yank got down, went through the house searching for arms. Two guns were given him and two pistols; he left the guns and one pistol, carried off a nice little one of Mr. George Batchelor's which would shoot six times. Vic begged for that, said it was hers, but he refused to let her keep it. He was joined by one [of] his comrades who had the most fiendish face in the world. Mr. and Mrs. Booth[2] rode up in the midst of it. Mrs. Booth's eyes were as large as saucers. The fiendish-looking Yank took out his greenbacks to show us – surprised because we did not express much wonder and astonishment mingled with admiration at his wealth, as he showed also a $20 bill. The first question they asked was, "Where are the horses?" How glad we were that they were in town. This evening a man from Wisconsin sat on the back steps and talked for a long time. He was more polite than the two in the morning; he said he scorned to steal. We did not credit all he said, by any means.

TUESDAY, MAY 19, 1863

This morning was spent in fear and trembling but no one appeared until three o'clock, when about a dozen ruffiantly looking fellows rushed into the house, first fastening their horses to the trees in front of the gallery – asked for arms, took both guns, one they carried with them, the other they order Fleming[3] to break. They went to the mill and stole 20 bushels of meal. We walked up to the gate this evening, saw no one; they are afraid to be out late.

WEDNESDAY, MAY 20, 1863

The Yanks came rather sooner today – several came this morning, with them a negro of Mr. Lanier's[4] who insisted that there were three grey horses here, told Mose[5] he had hid them; of course he could not produce them.

This negro spoke very impertinently to Mrs. Batchelor. She had ordered him to get out of the yard; he said he would go when his folks went. He asked her who she was talking to. She sent for an officer, a Mr. Short,[6] who was on the gallery. He went around, cursed the Negro – "You think you are free, but you are in greater bondage than you were ever before and if you [are] ever impertinent to a lady again" he would blow his brains out. He would act towards any man who would act in the same manner to a lady.

Mrs. Downs[7] rode over this morning in her carriage. We were delighted to see her as if she had risen from the dead. The same two ruffians who were [here] on Monday went to her house and searched for arms. For valuables, they should have said.

When they were here Vic and I went upstairs with them. They did not disturb anything in our room. We offered to show them [what was] in our trunks, but he said he would take our word for it, that we had nothing concealed. He said, "You all do not appear to be afraid of Yankees as some are." We told him we were not afraid. He was a little freckle-faced bowleg rascal. I am glad they found so little to satisfy them.

This evening Mrs. Batchelor and I felt emboldened by Mrs. Downs' visit to follow her example, so we got on the pony and Annie[8] and rode over to Sligo. We found Mr. and Mrs. Noland[9] looking dismal enough. The Yanks had been through Mrs. Noland's bureaus and wardrobe, taken her pins. Mr. Noland would not let her say a word or go around as we did. They were left to take what they pleased. He ought to have followed them at least to the smoke house. Mrs. Batchelor told the man, who came for meat, that if they took her meat and corn she would drive all of her negroes to their camp, as she would not be able to support them, and she did not want to see them starve. He did not take any but I suppose thought he would send somebody else who could have less conscience. They have treated her comparatively well. She talks firmly but politely to them. We also went over to Mr. Vaughn Noland's;[10] and they were glad to see us, ordered strawberries immediately.

Mrs. Noland had been extravagant enough to have her last turkey that day for dinner, the only one the Yanks had not stolen, thought it best to dispose of it. She invited us to partake of the remnants, which we did with pleasure. We stayed as long as we thought safe; on our way home we met Anderson[11] coming after us. Mr. Noland felt anxious.

Mrs. Noland sent for Parker[12] (whom he [Mr. Noland] had sent to town early Monday morning with his riding horse) to describe his meeting with the Yanks on his return from town. He met them, he said, about five miles from town. He thought they were our own soldiers. They asked him if he had a pass, he said he had. In pulling it out, he rattled some notes. He had one from Dr. Batchelor to Mr. Vaughn Noland and one from Dr. Booth[13] to his mother. The Yanks took possession of them, told him to tell his master and Mrs. Booth he would attend to it. Asked him where his master lived. "About five miles from the Baldwin Ferry[14] – Marse Pearce[15] lived three miles" from his Master. When they still did not know, Parker was astonished that they did not know where Mrs. Pearce Noland lived. He went on to explain but they d_____ all the rebels, and did not know where any of them lived. They asked him if he were not tired of riding, made him dismount. He had picked up a pair of boots on the road, which he had tied to the saddle, ordered him to take the d_____ rebel boots off. He was too slow, so the Yank took his knife and cut them loose. Yank mounted, and rode up and down. "This is a <u>heap</u> better than walking, I tell you, old man."

They asked him if he could cook.

"No indeed. Master says I am the meanest cook in the world. Master says I burn everything I attempt to cook. If you were to keep me here, I would pine to death, my poor children would pine for me."

While he was sitting there resting Ned Booth[16] came galloping up with his mistress' horse. The Yank stopped him, too.

"Have you a note, too?"

"Yes."

"Well, let me see it."

He took possession. "Well, tell your mistress I will carry her horses to Vicksburg. Take a seat by this old man."

Ned got off and took his seat.

Presently here comes a wagon filled with molasses from Vicksburg. They stopped that also, then a white man in a buggy with a barrel of flour.

"Get out and take a seat if you please."

Of course the man did so.

While they were talking to these men, Parker got up and left.

The Yanks had Mrs. Batchelor grinding corn all day yesterday.

Oh! how long, how long, will this last.

THURSDAY, MAY 21, 1863

This day is nearly ended – what a one it has been – long and weary indeed. Can the people in the North know or conceive what we suffer? We are tried beyond endurance, and suffer more than we can tell. We will be obliged to coin words to express our utter detestation of the hated. Can I ever visit the North again, with my present feelings, unnatural as they may be? I cannot ever go there again. I will not, my blood boils as I write, I can hardly write.

This morning about nine o'clock there came here about six men for chickens, etc. They were from the hospital, came for the chickens for the sick, ours as well as the Yankee sick and wounded. Mrs. Batchelor willingly gave up chickens and preserves for that purpose.

Mrs. Folkes[17] drove up in the midst. She was on her way to Mrs. Pearce Noland's to get Mrs. Alex Newman[18] to go home; she had been staying with her sister a week. Mrs. Folkes said the Yanks had destroyed everything about Mrs. Newman's place, had torn Mrs. Newman's clothes to pieces, had treated Mr. Newman very badly. Mrs. Folkes had as much news as usual. Mrs. Green[19] was staying with her mother. She says they took Dr. Newman[20] and carried him to the fortifications and back, that they threatened to whip Mr. Alex Newman.[21] Mrs. Folkes says she had met nearly all of the high officers in the Federal Army – Gens. McClernand,[22] Grant,[23] Osterhaus,[24] besides minor officers innumerable. One of Benton's[25] aids has taken a great fancy to Mrs. Green – a Col. Scott – told Miss Rebecca[26] that Mrs. Folkes was the very opposite of her beautiful sister. They carried our prisoners directly by Mrs. Brien's.[27] Mrs. Folkes ran out, determined to speak to them. The guard tried to keep her back, but she would go on; the prisoners cheered her, one soldier seized her and said he would kiss her. She said he must be satisfied with shaking hands. When she was leaving them she cheered for Jeff Davis[28] and she said she never heard such shouts.

Gen. Tilghman[29] was carried to Mrs. Brien's house at night by torch light. His hair was covered with blood. His son accompanied him. They thought at first of burying him in our church yard[30] but carried him to Vicksburg. Poor Gen. Tilghman – he was brave to a fault. We little thought a week ago when he passed this place that he would in so short a time be dead. I saw him last fall in Jackson, directly after his return from a prison at the North, Ft. Warren.[31] He made a speech at the Bowman House[32] and told us how cruelly he had been treated in prison. And now poor fellow, he is gone, but his name will live forever. He fell bravely defending his fireside and home. May he rest in peace.

The wretches have desecrated our beautiful church at Bovina. They have cut the organ pipes; they gave the prayer books to the negroes, among others Mrs. Batchelor's. One of the negroes gave it to Mrs. Folkes. She brought it down with her. How can anyone dare to desecrate the House of God. I wonder they were not afraid that their hands would be palsied in the attempt.

Immediately after dinner a dozen of the roughest specimens rode into the yard – Jim Lane's Jay Hawkers.[33] They came for meat, insisted that there was some hid, in which they were not mistaken, that some of the negroes said so at the quarters. We all denied it. Mr. Street,[34] who knew nothing of the matter, stood among them innocently indeed claiming that no meat was hid: "Gentlemen, this lady had none to hide." He hoped they were Christians. When I slipped around on the end of the gallery I heard them cursing and going on about the D__ned rebel women, who declared they had nothing hid, hiding all the time. Mr. Street was sitting with them, talking to them as benevolently as if they had been pinks of perfection. I told Mrs. Batchelor that we had better go around there for his protection. They did not have much to say when we were there. They soon went into the hen yard. The head man put his gun down on the ground and said, "There is something hid here." With two stokes of his ax, he struck the box. He soon obtained some spades and dug it up. They were disappointed at finding so little. Mrs. Batchelor went out and took all the blame on herself – said that the two negroes had only obeyed orders – that she did it to keep her family from starving and asked them if they would not have done the same. They said they would.

They then wished to search the house for imaginary treasure. They made an excuse that they must look for firearms. First they went into Mr. Street's room, then the parlor, Dr. Batchelor's room, upstairs into Mrs. Noland's room. They looked in all the trunks.

Vic and I took our seats in our rooms reading, determined to show them what was in our own trunks, but they did not intrude themselves there. Next went into the garret; my winter trunk was there with clothing in it. Mr. Street called for my key. I rushed upstairs perfectly furious, unlocked the trunk, tossed the things out, and asked if they were satisfied. They looked ashamed, as they well might do. I never was so nearly stifling in my life with rage. I told them the house had been searched already three or four times. I could have killed them with real pleasure. A week ago, could I have been convinced that my feelings would be as they are, that I would with pleasure, yes I believe I could kill them myself, with my own hands. At last they concluded to relieve us of their hateful presence, much to our relief. The negroes were perfectly furious.

Yesterday there was an officer here, who told Mr. Street that they heard he had hid some silver. Mr. Street said it was in Vicksburg.

"Take care old man how you talk."

Mr. Street said it was in Vicksburg.

We thought we had suffered enough for one day – and thought we would not be troubled again, so Vic, myself, and the children[35] concluded we would go down to the strawberry patch. We had hardly got down there when Mary and Sue[36] called us back. We jumped over the fence, rushed up the hill. When we reached the house they told us that a negro man had been galloping around the place with his gun cocked. He had then gone to the lot. Presently he and another negro came to the carriage house, ordered

Mose to pull the carriage out. Mose told them they must wait on themselves. They pulled it out, holding their guns the whole time; Anderson and Mose were on the watch to pick them up if they laid them down. One of the negroes was Mrs. Alex Newman's carriage driver. They said it was no use talking, they were bound to have that carriage. The negroes went out and talked to them. Gabe[37] pretended not to know Mary, but she convinced him that he did. They wanted someone to bring them water, but all refused. As they passed the quarters, Harris[38] stopped the carriage and told them something about Mary. On their way down the hill they met Myra with Lucinda;[39] they wanted them to get into the carriage. On Myra's refusing to comply one of them seized his gun, pointed it at her and Mary, who had run down the hill to save Lucinda, and fired. All was confusion and in a moment we imagined we were all killed, although no one was hurt. They called out that we might look out for them tonight to burn the house. All were frightened of course.

Just then we saw a wagon coming down the school house hill – a sutler's wagon, with two white men and a negro. We all in a body rushed out to beg help and protection in a very excited manner. The sutler sprang from his wagon, said he would do all he could, that there was a soldier in the wagon. The moment he heard what was the matter he jumped down and said he would blow out their brains. Anderson seized Mrs. Willis'[40] horse that was down at the quarter. The sutler soon followed, leaving the negro with his wagon in the yard. They have not yet returned. I hope they will soon.

What we are brought to, how humiliating. I feel that I cannot stand it. I am not afraid at all, but the disgrace almost – oh, it is horrible. Negroes rule the land. That wretch Gabe told Mary that Mrs. Newman and Mrs. Folkes were sitting on the road side, and might be thankful that no worse had befallen them. Poor women, how defenceless – Mrs. Folkes talking so bravely this morning. God help us. We are reduced down, down. How earnestly have we prayed, these last four days, that we might receive reinforcements, and whip them out.

FRIDAY, MAY 22, 1863

Last night a short time after we had gone to bed I heard a noise on the gravel. I said, "Vic, here they are."

"Oh! My god!" she exclaimed. "Light the candle."

The noise proved to be our protectors. They had come up with the negroes somewhere near Mrs. Newmans. The negroes had Mrs. Batchelor's carriage and Mrs. Tommy Brabston's.[41] They had stolen Mrs. John Brabston's[42] horses and put them on Mrs. Batchelor's carriage. The sutler and Mose came up on them; the soldier ordered them to harness the horses back to the carriage – they had taken the horses out. He in the meantime had taken possession of their guns. When he was not noticing the negroes they ran off as fast as possible, but Mose soon had all ready. He and Mr. John Brabston's driver mounted and together drove home rejoicing over restored property. I asked Mrs. Brabston's servant where Miss Mary Brabston[43] was. He said he had heard of her the day before; she was at Mr. Alex Cook's.[44]

The two white men remained here last night. This morning Mrs. Batchelor told them to go to the quarters and tell all the negroes who wished to go to the Yanks to pack up and go immediately. Kezziah[45] and some others who had made threats and acted very badly said they were not going, they would stay here. The soldier told them if he heard of any more fuss in the quarters he would come back and hang them. That quieted them but I do not know for what length of time. God grant we may not spend another such day as yesterday. Most of the Yanks we talk to say they are very tired of the war.

The sutler has mackerel, cheese, and other things of that kind besides calicoes, but I have not the slightest desire to possess any, even if I had the money. The sutler said Mrs. Newman told him to come in and look at her things. He says he never wants again to see such destruction.

LATER IN THE DAY

The soldier has kindly consented to stay all day with his gun and protect us; without his gun he would be powerless indeed. Did we ever think we should be so very glad to see, and persuade a Yankee to stay with us?

We have just had another scene. We act charades all day long – the curtain has always fallen at dark but we can with truth say "We do not know what an hour may bring forth." Several rascals came and were about to carry off Ellen's pony. This soldier, a Mr. Snyder, claimed him, but Kezziah said he was Ellen's. They would have taken him off – but Ellen went to them and told them it was hers, and the only way she had to get about. They then said they did not want it. They soon went down to the quarters when a message came for Jim.[46] Mrs. Batchelor and Mrs. Noland said they would go down and see what was to pay. Kezziah attacked her mistress and said, "You have had me beat enough," or something to that effect. Her mistress asked her why she did not go with the Yanks. She said she was not going, she wasn't going to leave her property. Her hatred for Fleming is terrible. She must feel in the situation of a "woman scorned" that the Book speaks of – horrible feeling, I should imagine. Presently Mr. Noland came running from the quarter and said Kezziah had raised her shovel on them and told them to leave. The soldiers, or rather dogs, I don't know what to call them, instead of protecting them against that fiend, grinned, perfectly delighted. Mrs. Batchelor did not leave in a hurry. She intends having Kezziah arrested and put in irons so soon as we can get a protector.

Old Charles[47] has gone with a letter written by Vic to Gen. Grant asking protection, not from his army, but from the marauding villains who prove that the only weapon they know of is might, who would tremble and run if a gun was pointed at them, dogs of the earth. This, Mr. Snyder says, "if their officers knew it, they would not allow it." Some might not, but others would encourage them.

Truly we need patience. May God shower it upon us. I have never been really frightened. I value my life but little but I would sell it as dearly as possible if these cowards were to attempt to take it.

Charles has just returned. He tried to get to headquarters but Gen. Grant had moved his quarters. He said no one troubled him. Some men asked him, "Which way, Uncle?"

"I belong to headquarters."

"That's right," they said.

He said he went to the two-mile bridge.[48] He says he never saw the like of the wounded men they had taken to Ferguson's house[49] for a hospital. Some of the men said Vicksburg is a hard place. He says the breastworks of cotton resisted all of their balls, they bound back, killed their own men. He says the sight of the wounded was terrible, legs and feet cut off – arms shot through, and wounded in every way possible.

Alfred[50] from Sligo and a boy from Yucatan[51] have just arrived to hear the news. Miss Mary[52] is staying with Mrs. Pearce Noland. Some of those thieves stole Mrs. Noland's and Ellen's breast pins yesterday in their raid for arms.

Guns heard today aplenty.

8 AT NIGHT

We have all remarked that it has been unusually quiet this evening, more like old times. We have had no scene. Jennie[53] has a chill and has now quite a high fever.

SATURDAY, MAY 23, 1863

Bombardment from Farragut's fleet,[54] it sounds like; commenced in the night. It is heard now at regular intervals. The people in the city must suffer. Why don't reinforcements come. The first day the Yankees came, Mr. and Mrs. Booth rode up. Mrs. Booth's eyes were a marvel to see; she grew perceptably larger by degrees. Mr. Booth was evidently trying to stifle his wrath.

11 O'CLOCK

We have had several visits this morning – they came on the neighbor's horses. There is a set at the quarters now – one of the party riding Andrew Bolls'[55] horse, and one, one of Dr. Newman's mules. They accused Mr. Noland of having been a commissary in our army, said a man told them so. Mr. Noland told them, for the Lord's sake, to bring that man here, but they refused. They rode around the yard. The same impertinent puppy who came on Monday was here. I cannot describe their looks and our feelings. While they are here, it is not fright but indignation that we feel. Oh! may we have strength and purpose to outlive these times; when they are here I feel no wavering nor fear, for that would do no good. If Vicksburg stands we can and will endure anything. But I know God will not desert us. He will not deliver us over into the hands of our enemies. Those Yanks said they nearly had Vicksburg yesterday; if the Colonel commanding a division had held out a half hour longer, they would have had possession. They expect to get into the city tonight – but God is good, He will not desert us.

There was a negro of Mr. Thompson's[56] here this morning with a Yank; he was on his master's riding horse, had his saddle and bridle. He was just from the battlefield, said Gen. Grant had sent a flag demanding the surrender of the city at 9 o'clock this morning – if refused he would burn the city.

The soldiers suspect this Mr. Snyder. He says he would not be surprised if they carried him to the camp on suspicion.

A note has just been received from Mr. Pearce Noland. He says Miss Mary went to headquarters yesterday but found that Grant was on the battlefield. She was treated politely and advised to go to Gen. Slack[57] at Big Black Bridge. Mrs. Brabston has sent [for protection] for herself; we are bound to have protection or else we will starve. Mr. James Brabston has an officer, and Dr. Newman. That is all untrue [what] we heard about Dr. Newman. One of his negroes, who was here this morning, said he was safe at home. "Hope deferred maketh the heart sick." Those dogs are at the quarters and sent two negroes for Annie Boylen.[58] Mrs. Batchelor sent them word they might have her, but they would be under the necessity of looking for her. They will remain at the quarters, and hear all kinds of falsehoods from the negroes, believing that they are poor creatures.

3 O'CLOCK

Miss Mary has just returned from Mr. Noland's. She is now on her way to the Bridge, appears to be delighted with her trip.

There were some men here today who were determined to find silver in the garden. One fellow with a gun went trampling all over it, knocking his gun down. He said his gun had something in it to find where something was buried.

6 O'CLOCK

Miss Mary has returned unsuccessful. She met Mr. Gibson[59] who told her to hurry on as Gen. Slack was on the move, that he had his protection papers in his jacket. We had given Miss Mary the letter we had written for Gen. Grant (No one saw anything objectionable in it) as she passed here. Well, she rode up to headquarters where the ex-colonel was with his staff around him, presented the letter. He did not like the contents, said if the lady wished protection she must use different language to the U.S. officers. Of course Miss Mary told him she did not know what was in the note. He waved the subject, was on the move, he is going to reinforce Grant at Vicksburg. He did not want to be troubled, that is the whole truth of the matter. I will copy the letter. Miss Mary heard that Gen. Grant had been wounded, shot in the arm. They say our men are just slaying the Yankees by the hundreds; the slaughter is terrific. Ferguson's yard is covered with the wounded, cotton bales are torn open for them to lie on. We heard that Gens. Carr[60] and Steel[61] were killed. I hope it may be so. I wish we could get into some of the Northern states and rob and destroy as we are now obliged to endure. Mrs. Batchelor sent to the officer at Mr. James Brabston's to give this Mr. Snyder power to protect us; he wrote one. The letter to Gen. Grant's letter was as follows:

[Editor's note: Parts of the next two pages of the diary are missing as a portion of Mrs. Batchelor's letter to General Grant was cut from the diary, presumably by Miss McKinley.]

" . . . time demand my rights of protection as a <u>lady.</u> Your soldiers came. They said for Arms. I handed them all that were in the house – and gave them my word none were hid. My words were to no avail. I spoke not to gentlemen but to <u>ruffians</u> and <u>thieves</u> who had no authority to act thus. My Daughter's trunks were not regarded, but opened, and contents thrown around. Every <u>pocket-book</u> and work box was opened to search for Arms. Three several times has my house been searched from Garrett to Cellar. I said not a word, though burning with righteous indignation. They came and took nearly all of my provisions, still I took it patiently – but now I have to tell you an act, that will make any gentleman <u>blush</u>. . . . "

[Editor's note: The reminder of the page is missing: the diary continues in mid-sentence.]

. . . came here, who says Gen. Hovey[62] sent him, that he had given the lady papers to the effect. Mrs. Batchelor told him she had none, that he was mistaken in the place. He did not appear to think so, being pleased with his quarters, but the admiration was not mutual. We were all anxious to get rid of him. He had no papers to prove his authority. Besides, we had Mr. Snyder here who had a paper.

While he was here he boasted of having been in Vicksburg yesterday but escaped, as all the men who with him assisted in taking a battery had been killed, that they had taken all of our breastworks but the last now, that Richmond had been taken, our papers lied, that they had taken thousands of our men prisoners, they did not want to fight and had come to them. Of course we did not believe him.

Presently up came a rough fellow on horseback. This Mr. Snyder asked him the news, if they were fighting today. He said only skirmishing – the great fight was on Sunday. We asked, "Are your men taking Vicksburg?"

"No, nor likely to take it soon."

The story teller said, "Why, some of our men were in Vicksburg yesterday."

"If they got in," he [Snyder] answered, "they slipped in."

"Any prisoners taken?"

"No chance of taking any. The rebels are behind their breastworks. They do not come out, and we can't get in."

He said two of their divisions had stormed a battery but the Rebels drove them back. The boaster said he went into the city with ten men, they all got killed but himself, and he made his escape bringing with him twelve prisoners – said that they could go in any time they pleased.

4 O'CLOCK

Before dinner today some men came into the yard asking to see Mr. Snyder's authority to protect this house. He showed it. They said it was alright but called Mr. Snyder to one side and told him that the negroes said we had meat and sacks of sugar hid. Mr. Snyder told them that they had found the meat, but as for sugar there was none he knew of. Presently up came the same set that stole the meat and asked if they could have dinner for eight. Mrs. Batchelor declined; steal all you have and then expect you to feed them! Impertinence does exceed.

Miss Mary has returned. Mrs. Dr. Newman went with her. They met Generals Grant, Hovey and Slack on their way to the Big Black. He told her he intended sending cavalry all around the country and drive the stragglers off. They had no business here at all. I will not believe it until I see it.

Miss Priss wrote a note to Vic. She told us of their first meeting with the Yanks. She and Chesley[63] ran down frantically to the gate on Monday morning to see the last of our pickets to go into town. Chesley exclaimed, "Are the Yankees far behind you gentlemen." Miss Priss saw in a moment who they were. "If my little sister had noticed your dress, her question would have been unnecessary."

This evening two weeks ago Mr. Phillipps[64] was here, rather later Mr. Gus Downs[65] came in, also Miss Mary Brabston; and Dr. Hicks[66] rode over. How changed now.

9 O'CLOCK

Mrs. Downs and Mrs. Young[67] came over this evening, brought a Yankee soldier on the carriage box to protect them. He said he was one of Gen. Smith's[68] bodyguards. He went to search for arms. Miss Mary went to Mr. Noland's this evening. Poor Mr. Hal Noland – they have completely robbed him of his clothes, bed linen and everything. Some men took his carriage – they said they would return it.

MONDAY, MAY 25, 1863

Vic and I went over early this morning to spend the day at Mrs. Downs; walked through the woods. We made Fleming and Sue go with us. We had plenty of visitors and rough ones, too. One man, an old fellow from Iowa, who entered the Army for his <u>health</u>, asked Mrs. Downs for flowers. She made him a bouquet. Capt. Young[69] gave him a letter to mail for him. He, Capt. Young, sometimes calls the men in, finds out their names and regiments and if they have behaved badly he promises to report them. A very rough looking set came there after corn, chickens, etc. Mrs. Downs told them she had some corn at Mrs. Brabston's, that if they intended taking her corn, she wished they would take that from there.

"Well, if we do will you give me dinner for eight? I will pay you for it."

She told them she did not have the meal, that she was cut off from her mill and had no cart to haul corn from Egypt.[70] They went off satisfied but said they must have dinner somewhere.

In the evening they returned, some taking their seats by the kitchen, others went into the garden and pulled up nearly all of the vegetables. We talked politely to the fellows, and as Mrs. Downs says every man has a soft place in his heart, we succeeded in finding theirs.

We walked home in the evening. When we reached the house, the first news that greeted me was that a man in the cavalry who had been sent out to clear the road of stragglers had inquired of the negroes for me, said he knew me in Tennessee. I know of but one man there who would remember me well enough to inquire and from the description it must have been him, but I thought better of him than ever to have suspected that he would be fighting in the Federal Army, as he is a Tennessean. If he ever comes back here I intend telling him that I heard he was in the graveyard and ask what he was doing there; we heard that a party had been digging in that region for silver. I will ask him if he has stooped that low.

Mrs. Batchelor has gone over to Sligo and Greenfield.[71] At the latter place she met Mrs. Booth who gave her an account of her troubles. Eight men took possession of her sack of flour. She rushed out, snatched it from them.

"You freckled face dogs. You shall not have my flour!"

She emptied the flour in a barrel, doubled up the bag, and pitched it at them. Sunday morning a ruffian fellow, whom his comrades called Butch, came to Mrs. Booth's and told her he had been all over her garden Saturday night, had heard her conversation with Mr. Booth on the gallery, had seen her put out the candle, and then [heard] their conversation in bed. He was looking for silver. He expected to find it, when he intended setting out immediately for Europe. He succeeded in finding the china, and had come to her with the request that she would come and help him bring it to the house as he wanted to see how it looked in the daytime. They carried it all in the house. Mrs. Booth told him if he got into Vicksburg he might have it; he said that he had heard that her son was in Vicksburg and when he got there he would make him get it. Mrs. Booth says Dr. Booth don't know anything about it.

TUESDAY, MAY 26, 1863

This morning has dawned gloomy – no arrivals yet.

4 O'CLOCK

Misery, did we ever feel it before! Party upon party have been here this day, some up here and some at the quarters. A party was here from the hospital for milk pans.[72] They took these; the principal surgeon left an order that no more should be taken. A party have just left; they took two wagon loads of corn, shot two sheep, and departed. Miss R.A.R.[73] has just sent me a note begging me to go with her to claim protection. We will go tomorrow.

FRIDAY, MAY 29, 1863

This morning the first sounds we heard was the booming of guns; we think they have been fighting desperately again. Yesterday and Wednesday we heard that Johnston[74] was at Snyder's Bluff.[75] I hope he is.

On Wednesday morning I rode over to Mrs. Downs to breakfast. Directly after we started, when we reached Dr. Newman's, who should come out but the Doctor, Mrs. Newman, and Mrs. Booth. Dr. Newman was going for permission to practice. We had a long ride, hot and dusty, for nothing. The General was on the battlefield. His son,[76] a boy of 12 years, was at headquarters. He was a good-natured looking boy – not smart. He ranks as captain on his father's staff.

We met plenty of officers. I have not yet met a gentleman among them. We remained some time talking. At the pickets, waiting to be attended to, their one question was, "Where is Johnston." We told them they ought to know better than we did.

Mrs. Booth had gone to Gen. McClernand to get protection. He told her he could not protect her as she had two sons fighting against the U.S. She went home and wrote one for herself. She drives the Yanks off with it.

When we reached Mrs. Downs we found Mrs. Folkes, Mrs. Green and Mrs. Hal Young. They came on a visit to Capt. Young. Mrs. Folkes had a fine bottle of brandy for him which she had made Gen. Sherman[77] give her. She went to Gen. Osterhaus for a guard the other day; he gave it to her but told her he would be obliged to send her to Ship Island[78] if she did not behave herself. She said if he did she would make bonfires of her kinky head, when we were victorious, as Mrs. Phillipps[79] did of pieces of candle.

Yesterday morning we started for the Bridge. We called to see Mr. Gibson. The Yankees had taken his cooking stove. He had a housefull all night.

They have ruined our church, destroyed the organ, shot holes through the walls, slit the Bishop's chair and we fear the portrait has been destroyed, but probably the Misses Bigelow[80] have it.

After passing Mrs. Evans'[81] place we came to some pickets who had received orders that day not to allow anyone to pass. We sent up word requesting an audience. When we obtained permission and were about going to see the General, a Col. Wright of the 6th Missouri stopped us and said after finding out our business they could not give us guards. They had their hands full now. I never met so rude a man in my life.

Major Marble[82] came riding along in a cart full of Yanks. He was seated in a chair. While we were at the pickets he had been walking. When they invited him to ride, he was about to pass through when they ordered him to stop. He got out and came to us, glad to be stopped. He said he stayed to hear the news in this neighborhood. He told us the Yanks had taken all of his clothes except the ones he had on. He was "dressed up" with his ruffled shirt and diamond pin. He says if he can have possession of his negroes for six months after the Yanks leave they may have them. He has yet fifty bushels of corn. He wanted to get protection for that.

Jim and Anderson have gone to the Yankees. They went they said to escape the draft. Anderson seemed very much mortified on his visit home, said he was coming back.

The Yanks found the silver last Monday evening.

We have seen but one or two Yankees today.

A terrible fight is going on this evening.

SATURDAY, MAY 30, 1863

Some Yankees arrived before we had hardly finished our breakfast. Gave them bread and milk. They told the negroes anybody could give a dog a better breakfast. Mrs. Batchelor charged them 50 cents a piece; they thought that enormous – wanted to pay her in cotton money.[83] I never saw such people. I think they are regular Yanks – stingy to the core.

Mrs. Folkes went with Mrs. Col. Cook[84] to Gen. Grant the other day. He would not give her protection. Mrs. Cook burst into tears and said she had always been for the Union, and opposed to secession, etc. Mrs. Folkes told her if she did not hush she would not ride home with her. Gen. Grant said he would send her home in a coach and six.

Mrs. Batchelor went over to Sligo this evening. We heard that the Yanks had taken Mr. Vaughn Noland and Mr. Hal Noland prisoners. Mr. Spears was home on furlough; he wished to hear from his mother.[85] Meeting "Old Billy,"[86] he gave him a note. Jack Black[87] informed the Yankees that Billy had a note for his Master Hal. They thought, I suppose, it might be some news from Hinds [County],[88] so a body of cavalry came and have taken him to Gen. Osterhaus. We expect them home this evening.

Just now there were two or three men drove up the cows and commenced milking. Mr. Snyder came up and drove them off. They told him they had seen a good many men like him, keeping out of the army and guarding rebel property. He told them they were about pretty business, taking from women and children their last mouthfulls.

8 O'CLOCK

While we were at supper six men rushed into the yard, hallowing each other, completely surrounded the house. You would have thought there was a thousand. We thought we were to be taken up bodily, house and all, but it was six Yankees on the lookout for four Confederate soldiers who they said the negroes told them were there. They took lights under the house, and through the house, every spot where you might imagine a man could get. At last they were satisfied, took their seats, and the "Orderly" commanding commenced a conversation. He told us sixty buildings had been burnt the night before. When we expressed our surprise at not seeing the light he informed us we could not see so far and was dumbfounded when we told him he was laboring under a mistake, that we saw readily every fire there. Then he told us how cruelly we treated their soldiers, and with what kindness they treated ours, particularly our officers, who were allowed to go at large, as they pleased. I reminded him of Gen. Tilghman and Buckner; he immediately changed the conversation, told us that the Confederates lost very heavily at Vicksburg. I wished to know if they could see into Vicksburg. We went to bed and left them. They very cooly fed their horses with corn from the stable. When they first rode up they said if the rascals did not come out they would shoot into the house and burn it down. I think they were somewhat ashamed of themselves. And all the commotion was caused because a negro boy told them there were soldiers here. I hope they will always believe what the negroes tell them; they will keep them trotting.

Miss Mary came from Mr. Pearce Noland's this evening and has been giving us a description of a visit they had from some officer who made a raid on the poultry, carried off all, young and old. One of them said he was an Abolitionist and his wife was worse than he.

SUNDAY, MAY 31, 1863

Heavy guns [have] been firing all the morning and in the night. Two weeks ago cannonading was on the Big Black. I wish it would commence again today. Vic and I went over to Mrs. Downs this evening to see Capt. Young. Mrs. Folkes and Mrs. Hal Young had been there spending the day. Mrs. Folkes has scraped up a relationship with Col. Hammond on Gen. Sherman's staff. She had his Ambrotype; she says he is about 27, but he is I think [in his] 40s. A Yankee also made her a present of a gingham dress, one he had stolen. Imagine, she had it on when we met her! She had no news. When she was at Sherman's quarters she told him she had assisted two Yankee deserters to get off. He told her he intended keeping her, ordered her horse put up. She told him she would walk home. He only intended frightening her.

Capt. Young is very much afraid of being sent to Camp Chase.[89]

Mrs. Downs gave us some very nice plums. Some of her negroes went up to Snyder's Bluff the other day to find if they could hear anything of Mr. Gus Downs, but nothing was heard.

Tonight a man (soldier) brought a note for Mrs. Batchelor from Mr. Gibson. They are going away – to Canada, I believe. Mr. Gibson says he is afraid of the effects on Mrs. Gibson's mind.

Tonight is a beautiful moonlight night, calm and still, except a curious quarrel going on down at the quarters between Flem and Kezziah. The last moonlight night a month ago, one Sunday evening I came from Mrs. Downs and found all here "down, down." They had just heard of our army's retreating from Port Gibson, Gen. Bowen's[90] brave men. We thought those were dark days, not believing that they could be so much darker.

2

"Their Impertinence
Is Unparalleled"

MONDAY, JUNE 1, 1863

This morning Mrs. Batchelor went over to Greenfield. They were all in fine spirits. Mrs. Booth had been over the evening before. Mrs. David Gibson's son,[1] a boy of about 12, was allowed to come out from Vicksburg to his mother. He says very few are hurt in the city. The people all have caves to run into and there is no thought of surrendering Vicksburg.

Some men have been here this morning.

1 O'CLOCK

Two Yanks have just arrived and asked for dinner. They are eating. After stealing all we have to eat, they have the presumption to come for dinner. Very few get anything to satisfy their appetites here, for they are refused, as they ought to be.

Mrs. Batchelor went to Mrs. Downs this evening, found all well. Just before tea three Yanks rode up and wanted supper, the same three that Mrs. Batchelor met at Mrs. Downs. Mr. Street told them that some of their kind were at the quarters eating supper. The spokesman of the party said they did not wish to eat with the negroes – the first ones that have not showed a decided preference for the "Americans of African descent." They also wanted corn for their horses, they would pay, did not wish to "sponge." Mrs. Batchelor told them she had nothing to eat for her own family, of course nothing for horses – they departed. I never imagined people could be so punished.

TUESDAY, JUNE 2, 1863

I am teaching today. No visitors yet. The same man who came for milk last night and took Henry Bolls'[2] bridle that he bought from a Yankee came back about dinner time and wanted milk. Mrs. Batchelor told him she did not have it. Then he said, "You must have drunk up a d____ sight since morning."

Their impertinence is unparalleled.

This evening Mrs. Annie Noland rode over on a poor old horse a Yankee gave her. He also gave her a paper telling her to keep him until he called for him. Of course he never intended doing that, and I do not blame him.

I hear the guns distinctly this evening, and I believe musketry.

They have taken Alice,[3] our last hope.

WEDNESDAY, JUNE 3, 1863

Today we spent at Mrs. Downs or rather with Capt. Young. Mrs. Downs sent horses for us. I rode with Miss Rebecca's new bridle a Yankee made and gave her. There were two crowds of Yanks there today, one a foraging party, half-starved they must have been, for they rushed into the smoke house and ate the raw meat, drank vinegar, rushed around seeking whom and what they might devour. Miss Rebecca told them she thought they were going to make a charge on us.

"Oh, no, we won't hurt you," one fellow said. [He said the South] "hauled off too quick." We should have waited to see what Old Abe intended doing, and the West might have hauled off with us.

One said the South was too proud to stay with the North.

Some of the best behaved came into the parlor with the request that we would play for them. Vic sang the "Bonnie Blue Flag;" they all admired that very much. One man remarked, "You ladies must not capture too many of our boys." Miss Rebecca told them we had soldiers enough to do that without our assistance. The red-nosed fellow who brought Miss Rebecca the bridle came back on a visit last evening. Had been to see Miss Phillipps. He is evidently struck either with her or Miss Rebecca. One man slipped into Capt. Young's room and was going off with a towel when Capt. Young called him back.

THURSDAY, JUNE 4, 1863

Mrs. Batchelor went with Mrs. Downs this morning to Gen. Osterhaus for protection. A set of wretches have just been here and taken off a barrel of sugar, and about twenty wagons have gone into the swamp after the corn there.

What will become of us I do not know. I pray God will visit these dev-ils with punishments equal to those they are inflicting on us. I would call down curses on their heads. I wish we had guerrillas so that these men could not so securely tramp around. I would willingly see my house burnt (if I had one) rather than see the wretches so secure from harm.

12 O'CLOCK

Mrs. Batchelor and Mrs. Downs have returned from Bovina[4] where they met Gen. Osterhaus who gave them both protection papers. They called at the Lodge[5] where four of our wounded men are. They found the Misses Powell[6] there. Poor fellows, one had had his leg amputated.

Mrs. Brien's house is a hospital. It is a perfect sight. I do not know how she manages to stay there.

The church has been a good deal injured, but not so much as we heard. The organ was not touched. The sick are lying in the church. The Bishop's portrait was cut to pieces, also his chair.

This evening we came to the conclusion that our clothes are disappearing and commenced a search. Found clothes stuffed under the planks upstairs and on top of Mr. Street's teister,[7] plenty of them, too, some with Sue's clothes wrapped around them. Sue was the thief. She has been behaving so well since the Yanks have been here that we hoped better things of her.

FRIDAY, JUNE 5, 1863

The children (Jennie and Agnes) went to Sligo this morning. The negroes have some rumors among them, that Fleming brought yesterday, about Gen. Johnston killing all the negroes. He says "hundreds came running into camp from Hinds to escape Johnston, tongues hanging out, perspiration streaming," etc. The negroes want some excuse to go to the Yanks so pretend to be greatly distressed and afraid to remain quietly at home, but refuse going with their only friends, the Yanks. Next week we will be doing our own work. Sue has been at the quarters all day. She is packing, no doubt, to be in readiness. Well, the sooner the better.

A Yank came in, about dinner time, to get his dinner. Mrs. Batchelor postponed dinner two hours, hoping he would leave, but he was determined to get what he came for. We think he is the very man who helped steal the silver and sent the word that they had found it. Mrs. Batchelor wanted to ask him what the men had done with it, but Mr. Noland would not hear of it. Thought of it very risky.

5 O'CLOCK

Mr. Vaughn Noland has just been here, rode a mule. The mule with the saddle and bridle belonged to a negro; he had borrowed them for the occasion. He and Mr. Pearce Noland had been that day to see about drawing rations. At Mr. Cooper's[8] he put all the families names down, all went today to get their provisions. Mr. J. N.[9] and Mr. Webb[10] went. Mr. Noland did not fancy going much.

SATURDAY, JUNE 6, 1863

Anderson came home last night sick. This morning Vic and I went to the quarters to see Sue. We found Eliza[11] on the floor mending clothes. Sue heard that they were going to the Yanks. We were anxious to keep Sue if possible. I do not think she is anxious to go, but so very much mortified and ashamed (not penitent) at her bad conduct that she felt as if she could not stay here, and of course had not courage enough to face the negroes in the yard and show by her conduct that she intended to do better, but she and her mammy prefer sinking deeper into the mire. Negroes are creatures you cannot convince but in some ways like children. It is useless to argue with them. Do what you think right and your duty – regardless of what they think.

An old man from Wisconsin was here this morning, a Mr. Garner. He was formerly a flatboatman, knew every other man in Amite.[12] Ten men also came for dinner but failed in getting any.

SUNDAY, JUNE 7, 1863

We hear cannon and musketry now and have heard it all the morning. I hope it is Johnston. We heard yesterday through a gentleman of this neighborhood that he was crossing at Satartia.[13] There must be something more than usual, for we hear musketry constantly. Miss Mary walked from Mr. Pearce Noland's last evening. Mrs. McGaughey[14] and family are there. On Friday while Mr. McG had gone to draw his rations (he left a young Mr. Brick[15] with his family) his negroes came to the house to whip Mrs. McG. Mr. Brick defended her as long as he could, but finding himself overpowered, he told her to run for her life. She and the children, seven in number, ran in all directions. Johnnie McG[16] met two Yanks and told them in heavens name to hurry on as the negroes were killing young Brick. The Yanks pretended to be enraged, put ropes around some of the negroes necks, carried them off, promised to hang them, but took good care to release them in the woods. One negro woman was shot in her knee. She said Mrs. McG had better leave as the negroes said they were coming again. When they got Mr. Brick down, they whipped him and made him call them <u>Master</u> and <u>Mistress</u>.

MONDAY, JUNE 8, 1863

Vic and I went to Greenfield this morning, found all well, came back about ten o'clock and found Mr. Pearce Noland here, who had ventured out three weeks ago this evening. He came up on his black horse to hear the news. We greeted him with "The Yankees have been here." "Where, when!" were his exclamations. It did not take us long to explain; he darted home. The Yanks soon paid him a visit. He rode this morning a poor animal he had picked up somewhere. Vic and I rode horses that Mr. Webb brought from camp. Very good matches, if they could be kept, but a Yank was about to carry them off today when Anderson told him they belonged to soldiers. He was satisfied – and so were we. Mr. Webb returned from camp bringing the rations he had been after for the last three days – 75 pounds of flour, 2 pounds of coffee, soap, 2 candles, etc.[17] He is going again on Wednesday.

A man calling himself an enrolling officer came this evening and carried off the three remaining negro boys, aged 12 - 14 - 16 years – soldiers, I suppose – "Old Charles" too. Glad to have an excuse to go, I think.

TUESDAY, JUNE 9, 1863

Vic and I went over to Mrs. Downs yesterday evening, found that Capt. Young had gone to Dr. Newman's and Miss Rebecca to Mrs. Brabston's. Mrs. Downs was at home. She gave us a description of her visit to Gen. McPherson's[18] quarters the other day. She says he was fixed so nicely in his camp. She told [him] she thought he proposed staying all summer. He said he did.

They say Miss Mary Brabston is the most unhappy looking girl – seems to have sunk into a settled melancholy. She cannot get home. She once said she would rather die than lose her property. I always thought she had more strength of mind than to allow the loss of worldly goods [to] affect her in the manner they say it does. She has her health, and education, which the Yanks cannot take away. I am sorry for her.

The same Mr. Garner who was here on Saturday came last night. He brought Ellen a horse. He is a most miserable looking animal but I suppose will improve.

Mr. Snyder went to camp yesterday morning but returned late last night. He brought Mrs. Batchelor some cheese and a nice pair of shoes. He said the men were greatly demoralized. Kirby Smith has whipped the Yanks badly at Milliken's Bend.[19] He said the men were low spirited.

Martha Miller[20] on her way to camp yesterday stopped with the Yanks in Mrs. Downs' garden, helped herself to vegetables, and went her way rejoicing. Such conduct is unbearable but her day will not last long. John Brick brought word from camp on Sunday that Catherine[21] was homesick, that when she met him she cried like a child and said she regretted ever having left home. Martha Miller contradicted this and said Catherine was very happily fixed in a house in Yazoo City. Of course the negroes believe the report most favorable to themselves.

The Yankee papers all acknowledge that Vicksburg is a great trial on their patience, but the last report is they are sure to have it in 48 hours. Gen. Grant intends blowing up the city, our Generals all being asleep in the meantime. Poor Grant – how bitter must his disappointment be. He imagined himself a hero of the war. He would march straight into Vicksburg and be worshiped ever afterward by all the faithful citizens of the North. But he is doomed to disappointment.

We have heard that there has been a fight at Port Hudson.[22] Among others there was a negro regiment of which 600 were killed. I am afraid Banks' Corps D'Afrique[23] will prove a failure.

Mrs. Batchelor and Mrs. Downs have gone to Bovina to see the Provost Marshal, also the Confederate soldiers at the lodge – carried them something to eat. When they went there the other day they found Misses Powell and Bigelow. Miss Powell said she had heard the report Mrs. Folkes was circulating of her father having taken the oath. That is a story, and she would make her answerable for it.

Mrs. Booth spent part of the evening here – gave us an account of herself since we saw her last. She has seen little of them for the last ten days.

She had been to see Dr. Nailer,[24] who is still in [custody] and has not the slightest idea what he is kept for. Gen. McClernand detains him, but she (Mrs. Booth) says it is entirely the adjutant general's doings. Dr. Nailer is very much pleased with the General. He (Dr. Nailer) is obliged to do his own cooking and makes his own fires. They want him to take the citizens oath,[25] the same which Mr. Lanier and Reese Cook[26] have taken. He says his bones may "bleach on this hill before I take it." The day before his wife had been to see him. She was very distressed. He, to try her, told her as she was so much distressed, he thought he had better take the oath. She exclaimed, oh, no she would rather he die first. He is obliged to associate with the low-down ragtag of the army, and if it were not for two other gentlemen with him, in the same predicament as himself, he would grow desperate. Mrs. Booth says she would not be surprised to hear of their carrying him off North any time. The adjutant general told her they never allowed a citizen to return if they once got within Gen. McClernand's lines. She even went to see Gen. Grant on his behalf, but he told her he could not interfere, it was beyond his province, that Gen. McClernand certainly had some good reason for detaining Dr. Nailer. She says the Provost Marshal gave her a paper of protection, also a paper to get back two ladies saddle horses, her own "personal property," also a right to keep them. While she was there two deserters from Vicksburg were brought in. The Provost Marshal questioned them; they were Dutchmen from Texas. He asked "How are they for provisions, how much meat do they get?"

"So much," measuring about three inches on his hand.

"More than that?"

"So much," (half a hand).

"Yes."

"How much bread?"

"About a foot's length."

"Have they plenty of ammunition?"

"Yes, full."

"How much?"

"Forty rounds."

Mrs. Booth thought she would question them: "Any women and children killed?"

"None, we did not see any."

"I heard there was a large fire the other night, is that so?"

"We don't know, we did not see it. We heard a block had been burnt, about the middle of the city."

Everything had to be drawn out of them. They were two poor stupid fellows who did not want to fight so deserted.

Mrs. Batchelor and Vic returned while Mrs. Booth was here. They had quite a difficult time getting here. The Yanks had blocked up the road. Vic was obliged to get off her horse and put down the fence. Mrs. Batchelor, Mrs. Downs, and Mrs. Brabston had seen the Provost Marshal. He was polite, promised Mrs. Downs he would send her a guard. They did not see the General. Henry Bolls rode over this evening. The three Mr. Nolands were here; no news. Vic, Miss Rebecca and myself are going to see the Confederate soldiers at the lodge tomorrow. Mrs. Batchelor stopped at Mr. Cook's to see Mrs. Brabston and Miss Mary. They looked disconsolate enough. They had obtained a pass but Mrs. Brabston was doubtful about going. She did not want to leave her home, wanting to know if she came home, if her neighbors would help her go to housekeeping.

WEDNESDAY, JUNE 10, 1863

This morning I woke up with the sound of rain pattering on the gallery roof – delightful sound as we have not had rain for a long time.

The Yanks keep shelling – at least we hear guns.

I have been teaching and reading all day. I have just finished "The Days of My Life."

Mr. Vaughn and Hal Noland came over this evening.

Some thieves went around the country and drove off the few remaining cows people had. They left six cows here, drove all off from Sligo.

THURSDAY, JUNE 11, 1863

Firing again this morning. Vicksburg not taken yet.

Dr. Newman is downstairs. I wonder if he feels any more hopeful than he did in former times.

Mrs. Noland has a daughter. I wonder what she will name it.

5 O'CLOCK

About twenty Yankees have been here since one o'clock. They came to blockade the roads, have cut down two large trees on the hill. They insisted on having some milk. Mrs. Batchelor told them that they could not expect her to give them milk when they had driven off all her cows. The Lieutenant spent about an hour in Mary's house – told Mary if she would go with him he would fix her as comfortable as he had Catherine. Mary told him that he was in a bad box. This is Lucinda's report. He afterwards called on Louisa and Myra. He is doing all he can to persuade them off, and when leaving he took Johnnie[27] up behind him on his horse – said he was going to take him as he wanted to go. We insisted that he should be left. Johnnie wanted to go. I told him I would tell his daddy that he wanted to go with the Yankees. Mary had to chase Johnnie down the hill after the man had put him down. She gave him a good whipping.

There was quite a nice Yank sat on the gallery and talked. He said men did things in the Army they would be ashamed to recall hereafter.

There was a fellow at Mrs. Downs told Miss Rebecca and Vic that there was a new general in command of Vicksburg. They inquired who, he said Gen. "Starvation." They told that they (the Yanks) had a general but not a new one, Gen. "Steal." We hear that Gen. Johnston is crossing at Hall's Ferry – I hope it may be true. I know he will not attempt to cross without he has a large force. We daily and hourly wish for him.

I would like to see that same squad of men compelled to cut those trees out of the road. I wonder sometimes if they do not spit liquid fire, like Asa Hartz' Devils.[28] I believe I will watch.

Mr. Webb and Mr. Noland have returned without rations. Mr. Noland says he will not go anymore. The Yanks say they are tired of feeding Jeff Davis' children. Letty[29] asked one of them if he were not afraid of Johnston.

FRIDAY, JUNE 12, 1863

Mr. Webb returned from camp without rations. No news, very little firing.

This evening a crowd under Sgt. McKitty came into the back yard by the cistern. The Sergeant came on the gallery and took his seat. He prides himself on being a gentleman so we abuse him as much as we please; he can do nothing.[30] He says he intends coming here on Sunday – for us to take him prisoner. His lieutenant, the same that was here before, spent part of his time with Mary – and then concluded he would pay us a visit. Mrs. Batchelor had made Johnnie take his seat behind her as he (the lieutenant) had taken a great fancy to him and wishes to adopt him. No one noticed him, but Mr. Street, who got up, shook hands with him, handed him a chair. We were all silent.

"I have come to get that little boy," was his sage remark.

We said not a word. He sat a while and then left. Then Sgt. McKitty said there was a young lady down here he had heard the lieutenant was very much pleased with, a Miss Mary. He wanted to know which of us it was. I told him it was not a young lady – it was a servant. He opened his eyes in astonishment. The men in the meantime were cursing and running around playing. The dogs.

SATURDAY, JUNE 13, 1863

This morning early a set of Yanks came for the last corn. Mr. Snyder went to them, showed the Genl's papers, they said d_____ his papers. Mr. Street went up to them and talked to them. They promised they would take but one wagon load (but of course they can not tell the truth), that they were ordered this morning to take the last grain of Mrs. Bolls' corn. Mrs. Batchelor is going to Mrs. Downs' this evening to ask her to go to Gen. Osterhaus and ask him why his papers are not more respected. They are still at the General's house.

We heard yesterday evening that one of [the] Confederate soldiers at the lodge was dying. Poor fellow, away from his home in Missouri, but he must have the consciousness that he has done his duty.

A man came today after Mrs. Batchelor's log wheel. He was polite, promised to return it.

A fellow came this evening, said President Davis was in Vicksburg, that the Yanks would soon have Vicksburg, that Pemberton had been out under a flag of truce and told them so.

Three cavalrymen were here and left a short time ago. They came for something to eat but did not get it.

Mr. Noland and Mr. Webb have returned from camp with their rations. Mrs. Batchelor is going to Gen. Osterhaus. Useless.

SUNDAY, JUNE 14, 1863

This morning at six o'clock Jennie and I started to walk to Mrs. Vaughn Noland's. Walking at a moderate pace, we arrived about half an hour before breakfast. I did not feel at all tired. We saw the baby a few minutes after our arrival. It is a very pretty young baby. Mrs. Tigner[31] is quite sick. Mr. Noland had sent twice the day before for Dr. Newman, but he was too unwell himself to come. Poor people – one physician for the whole country – Dr. Nailor in prison, the doctors in Vicksburg cut off – it is horrible to think of.

Mrs. Noland sent for Mrs. Booth early in the morning. She came over and prescribed [medicine and treatment] for Mrs. Tigner. I declare, she is a good neighbor; she (Mrs. Booth) proposed sending her horse for Mrs. Batchelor. Jennie started on the horse, met Mrs. Batchelor and Mrs. Noland riding and Mr. Noland walking. He took Jennie's horse and she walked the rest of the way home. They soon arrived. Mrs. Batchelor and Mrs. Booth remained all day, and myself. This evening they sent for the horses for us. I rode a horse that had a colt – Mr. Webb's horse. She would stop every three minutes to see if her colt was coming. When we got to the gate at the Sligo overseer's house we met some Yanks. Behind some distance we came to a man who stood holding his mule, looking disconsolate enough. These men made him go off with them. He has been looking for some men in Oster- haus' division to keep out of the Army but has been quite sick, was home until he recovered. They would not listen to his story, made him go with them. We told him to come go back with us. He rode along until he came to the woods, where he slipped off on his mule and went into the woods. After a while the gentleman came back for him but he was nowhere to be found.

The Yanks have found all of Mrs. Lane's[32] silver, also Mrs. Sexton's[33] and her jewelry, all buried. Took Mrs. Frank Gibson's[34] dead son's clothing, which she had kept for years. Mrs. Tully Gibson[35] started for Virginia to join her husband the Wednesday morning after the Yanks had taken possession here, in her carriage with her little boy and two demoralized servants. Her friends here have not heard a word from her. Her servants may have mur- dered her for her money.

We heard this evening that fifteen of the Yankee cavalry had been cap- tured on the other side of the [Big Black] River and that the Yankee army slept on their arms every night. I hope those miserable boasters, Lieutenant Meise, Sgt. Anderson and McKitty are among the members captured.

There has been a big of commotion in the quarters. A negro woman gave her daughter a whipping, at least that was her desire, but the daughter resisted. I do not know who finally conquered. Fleming gave his ex-wife

Kezziah a <u>thumping</u> as she threatened to poison [him and] told him roman-
tically that if he would not live with her he should not live with anyone else.
I do not know if it was her intention to die with him or continue to live for
a more deserving death (a hanging). The last news from the negroes is that
the Yanks say – and every word they believe – that those thieving soldiers
were <u>Confederate</u> soldiers, not Yankees. Oh no, they would not hurt the
poor negroes.

MONDAY, JUNE 15, 1863

We hear a little firing this morning. A Yank was here this morning, one
of the same who came Saturday evening. In the course of the conversation,
he said the Yanks might as well use the negroes as for their owners to use
them against the Yanks. We said it had never been done. He said he had seen
regiments in Van Dorn's Cavalry.[36] Of course we differed. It was besides a
very poor argument for anyone has more right to use his own property as
he wishes than his enemy could have. He brought a paper for Mr. Noland.
He is fighting for the old Union, approves of all of old Abe's doings. He
has a precise way of talking, like Mr. Short, after the same order, I suspect.

Mrs. Batchelor is quite unwell today.

TUESDAY, JUNE 16, 1863

I went over early this morning to Greenfield, spent the day. Mrs. Tigner
is quite sick. Mrs. Noland wanted me to stay the night, but I came back and
sent Miss Mary to spend the night. Capt. Young came over this morning
with Mrs. Downs. Mrs. Batchelor has been in bed all day.

WEDNESDAY, JUNE 17, 1863

Mrs. Noland went today to spend the day with Mrs. Tigner; she is still
quite ill. Mrs. Batchelor is better. About eleven o'clock four Yanks walked
very politely up to the house, asked for the master of the house. After talking sometime with Mr. Street they told him that they had to search the cisterns for arms. Mr. Street politely invited them round. They looked down,
imagining that they might see them either floating on the surface or shin-
ing down in the bottom but were doomed to disappointment as they have
been before for they only saw their own ugly faces reflected. Capt. Young
went out and expostulated with them, (first asking to what regiment they
belonged, etc.). They told him they respected him as a Confederate officer
but that they were not interfering with what belonged to him. He threatened to report. They did not care a d____n (favorite expression). One man
told him (Capt. Young) that he would like to have the charge of him for a
while. Vic and I in the meantime were on the back gallery carrying on a
general conversation with the men, Mr. Street and each other. Mr. Street
told us to go in, said Vic had a long tongue, was furious with us. We knew
the consequences and yet determined to brave his wrath. He insisted on
calling them gentlemen. Capt. Young said it was a burlesque on them; we

sneered, Mr. Street fumed. They departed, two of their number to the quarters to bring the poles, put them in [the cistern], felt around, found nothing, of course. They then felt in the other cistern and promised to come this evening to search the house.

Mr. Snyder has gone to his camp. Mr. Street, after their departure, came in, gave us a long talk, told us we would succeed in getting the house burnt. Vic asked the Yanks to tell her honestly if they ever had found any arms in cisterns. They said they had found a box of pistols in one not far from here. Verily Uncle Sam has men devoted to his cause. They do not allow a single leaf unturned or a crack peeped into where there might be the slightest chance of hooking something. ("I intend to write a book for the succeeding generation's benefit that never try to hide anything from a Yank unless you have some way of sending it to Heaven." – Vic).

Mrs. Booth and Miss Mary rode up in the midst, Mrs. Batchelor searching for her cows, which had been stolen, while she was on a visit to the sick, Mrs. Noland and Mrs. Tigner. Mrs. Booth sent her word, so she mounted in haste and pursued. I hope she will be able to find them. I declare it is almost ludicrous to think of. The other day Mrs. Downs told a Yankee officer who was eating his dinner at her house, while his men were rushing furiously around the house shooting the poultry, that these were terrible times to live in.

"Yes, they are rather uncomfortable."

"Uncomfortable!" exclaimed Mrs. Downs. "That word does not give any idea of the times at all."

Monday evening Vic and I rode over to see Mrs. Downs. She had been that morning to see Gen. Grant to obtain protection papers for Henry (her servant). He gave them to her. Now no one can trouble him; he is delighted. She saw the General himself – says his tent was very plainly furnished. She told him that he was not so well fixed as some of his officers. He told her he did not approve of luxuries.

A man told us a good joke on a colonel of the 6th Missouri. He was on picket when he saw [at] a distance in the dusk of the evening some of his own men who were blockading the roads. He sent couriers to Gen. Grant that the rebels were approaching in large numbers.

FRIDAY, JUNE 19, 1863

Yesterday I spent at Mr. Vaughn Noland's, sat up the night before, walked here last evening.

Today Vic and I went to the Provost Marshal. George Hawkins[37] went with us. We were stopped at the picket post; one of their number said he would go and see the Provost. He returned with him while we were waiting. We sat on a rail which one of the Yanks fixed for us and talked to them. They all look forward with so much pleasure to the fall of Vicksburg when they expect to be ordered home. Every regiment expects to be the favored one. We asked an Ohioan if he would not like to see his fellow statesman,

Vallandigham.[38] He said he would, to put a ball through him. We told them of Leonard Wood's[39] speech in New York. They had not seen the papers. Of course we do all we can to demoralize them.

After the Provost came to us, we stated our business, which was to get Vic's horse and Alice, which we knew were in Osterhaus' division. We described them and are to return in a day or two for them. We will go on Sunday. The Provost told us he had spent two years in the South. We told him he visited it at rather unfavorable times. He said he did not want to come at this time but was made to do so by the Rebels. Vic told him he was very much mistaken, that we did not want him and wished he and all present were at home. He was much amused and said she was candid. He appeared to be a gentleman.

We then rode to the lodge to visit the Confederate sick, but they had been removed, some to the Misses Bigelow and the others to Mrs. Brien's. We rode to our Church which is now a hospital to buy some brandy for Mrs. Batchelor who is still quite sick. The surgeon in command came out to see us, gave us the whiskey, divided with us – said they had about thirty men. They have them in arbors now in the yard. Said there was one had just died and another dying. They were making a coffin for one while we were there. They were buried in different parts of the churchyard to be disintern hereafter by their friends. Mr. Woodson, a Confederate who died at the lodge a few days ago, was buried in the graveyard somewhere.

We had a hot ride home, I on a trotting horse, Vic on a mule. We found Mrs. Batchelor quite unwell and disappointed because Dr. Newman had not been to see her. Mr. Street had been entertaining her in our absence on her bad looks, not very comforting news when one is sick.

We have heard this evening that our men in Vicksburg came out of their trenches and gave the Yanks fight last night, which accounts for the musketry we heard. I hope they did them immense harm. We also heard that Johnston and Grant had had a fight on Monday up on the Yazoo.

In looking over a "Harper's Weekly" this evening, I see that at Barnum's there is a painting which is causing quite a furor. It is a representation of "John Brown"[40] on his way to his execution when he meets the negro woman with her "babe." He stops and kisses it "tenderly." The officer in command scowls on him and pushes her aside. The comments are graphic on the poor Africans and John Brown <u>sacrificing</u> his life for them.

SUNDAY, JUNE 21, 1863

This morning I came from Mr. Vaughn Noland's and took my breakfast here [at Mrs. Batchelor's]. Vic and I then started for the Bridge, passed through as the Provost had given us a pass. We kept the straight road for Mrs. Spears' – did not see many men in front of Mrs. Spears' house. The U.S. flag was waving. We did not notice it but made our way to the Provost who was standing near the house. He joined us, told us he had not been successful in his search for the horse. He knew that a pony was in the division but not the other horse – did not yet have the pony for us. I thought when I first met him that he was of the kind to readily promise but not perform. I was convinced of it then. We saw a number of horses tied around. In a moment Vic said, "Miss Emilie, there is my horse." The Provost said let us go and look at it. As soon as we got near, we found that it was Sumter, pointed out to the Provost the bullet mark in his shoulder, also the brand of P.N.

The Provost went after the then owner of the horse. He did not make his appearance but the Provost returned, with him a Major somebody. Also one or two gentlemen stepped up, looked at us, then at the horse.

One fellow said, "So he was wounded, oh – of course he was."

I could have told him, "and I bet you were the man who stole him."

We had George Hawkins with us. He and Vic dismounted. George exchanged saddles from the poor pitiful looking pony she had been riding to Sumter, and very glad she was to make the exchange. The Major said he supposed the horse was not named for the Massachusetts man[41] of that name; we assured him of the contrary.

I thought I would try and get Wood.[42] I told the Provost that the horse was in the Third Illinois; he said he represented the regiment. He said we might have him, but of course we will never see him. We told them Sumter had been wounded at Champion's Hill, that Vic had lent him to Capt. Young. The Major said, "Well, Captain, I think this horse must be confiscated; he is government property." Vic said they would be obliged to confiscate her if they took her horse. So much the greater inducement, said the Major gallantly (as he thought). The Provost said he had been intending to come down in the neighborhood but had not had time. He proposed to the Major to ride with us then, but as we did not second the proposal, they did not accompany us. I am very sure I did not want their company. The Major said he had heard that Miss Batchelor was the Belle of the County – had heard Miss Newman speak of her.

We took our leave after first getting a pass to go out. We passed the picket posts before reaching Bovina. When we reached there we concluded we would go and see the Confederate soldiers at Misses Bigelow. They had two or three sick there. We went in to see them. One was shot in the leg, a Mr. Finley from Missouri, the other in the head, from Georgia. It was really refreshing to see some color besides the everlasting blue the Yanks wear. We stayed some time talking with them.

When we had passed Mr. Johnson's[43] going rather fast, Vic on Sumter and I on a mule, we heard someone shouting to us to stop. It was some time before we knew that they were talking to us. They were pickets. The officer said it was a disgustable duty he was performing. We told them we passed the pickets on the other road. They examined our pass and let us go.

The officer was on his way to Baldwin's Ferry, would ride with us if we had no objections. He talked of the sad state of the country, that he was a Kentuckian and did not approve of Lincoln's proclamation, did not like this making soldiers of the Blacks, would lead to servile insurrection, detested this making war on women and children. If it continued he would resign and go home. He was a War Democrat. He would like to see the Union restored as it was, but not [if the South] was unwilling to be united, as it would be no union. Thought the Cotton States were rather hasty in seceding – [should have] waited awhile and all gone out at once if necessary. We asked him what he thought of McClernand's being suspended. Said he did not like it. He himself belonged to his Corps, but he said he understood why it was done. McClernand was too popular a man, that he had been too successful. His neck must be trampled under for the sake of Grant, that McClernand was really the author of their success in this state. He gave us his name – Capt. Treadway of the 7th Kentucky.

When we reached home, we found Mrs. Booth, Mrs. Downs and Miss Rebecca here. Mrs. Downs insisted on Vic and I going home with her but we declined. When they reached the foot of the hill, they had met their guard with a note from Capt. Young to Mrs. Downs telling her that he had some Yankee officers on a visit to him who were splendid musicians. They were singing at that time. He sent to her to hurry home and bring us with her. We hesitated and refused to go at first, but Mrs. Batchelor insisted on our going, said she would do well without us, so we went, found the Yanks in full possession of both piano and melodeon. They sang all the evening, as much for their own amusement as ours. They sang the "Le Deum," "Gloria in Excelsis," and "Benedicti" besides numerous hymns – beautifully.

Julia said,[44] "Just listen to those Yankees singing our hymns." She was very indignant.

A Captain sang a song, "The Death of Ellsworth,"[45] the air was beautiful. They sang some other ballads. All had fine voices. They remained to dinner, told enormous stories. We told them we had heard direct from Vicksburg, that there had been two citizens killed and only two hundred soldiers. We told of the caves they had there. One fellow said it would be a nice place for them to keep their butter in. Capt. Young told them they would eat many pounds before they kept it in Vicksburg.

Mrs. Downs would not go to dinner, made Miss Rebecca and I go, said she did not want to sit at the head of a table when she had no better dinner (It was a very nice one, much too good for them). We told her she ought not to give them anything as they had stolen all we had. She wanted them to see that she could have a nice dinner, not on their account but on her own. After dinner they sang again.

While we were at dinner a surgeon and Major Adams came to see Capt. Young. Vic and I did not remain in the parlor very long. We went into Mrs. Downs room. The servants at Mrs. Downs were very indignant (They have been more loyal than any in the neighborhood). Caroline[46] said we were just wrapped up in the Yankees. Some said Miss Rebecca thinks more of them than she does of our soldiers. She laughs and jokes with them all the time. Julia[47] was furious because she had to cook for them.

I think Mary will leave in a few days. Henry Downs[48] says she has been talking about going. He told her she must leave Johnnie with him.

Capt. Young rode home with us. Found Mrs. Batchelor quite unwell.

MONDAY, JUNE 22, 1863

Monday evening I went to Mrs. Noland's and remained all night. Yesterday morning Mrs. Downs and Miss Rebecca with Mrs. J. Noland came over. We all moved Mrs. Tigner into the parlor. Mrs. Batchelor is much better. Mrs. Downs said if I would go home with Miss Rebecca she would stay with Mrs. Batchelor all day. Of course I went, played three games of chess with Capt. Young, beat two of them.

Miss Mary Brabston rode with Dr. Newman. She is looking very well. I was very glad to see her. Mrs. Green and her little boy rode down to see Mrs. Batchelor. She told us that Mr. Aleck Newman tried to kill himself the other day (We knew that he was crazy) by attempting to cut an artery in his arm. She also told us that Mrs. Folkes had been found straying around the battlefield at Bridgeport[49] on Monday by the Yankees, so they carried her home and put a guard around the house. She acts very foolishly. Dr. Newman calls her the Widow Folkes.

The Yanks took possession of young Albert Newman[50] last week. He had crossed the [Big Black] River from his uncle's on his way home but unfortunately asked the pickets a number of questions. They took him up on suspicion, carried him to headquarters. Mrs. Booth and Miss Sally[51] went up to try and secure his release but were unable. He is at McClernand's quarters. A Yankee officer told Miss Rebecca he had unintentionally been the means of making a friend of his a prisoner from Vicksburg. He says he sent him a word to meet him in a certain place on the railroad I believe, as they were old friends. In the meantime he was obligated to leave the spot designated. The friend from Vicksburg came out unsuspectingly to meet him when lo and behold he was taken up by a picket and carried to Grant. The Yankee who had gotten him into the difficulty explained matters to the General who said the gentleman might be released but he had seen too much. He should not be held as a prisoner. Mrs. R. says the Yank appeared very much mortified and ashamed while he was telling it.

Big guns are heard now. It is supposed that they are fighting at Bridgeport. Mrs. Booth sent word that Johnston was crossing the river last night.[52]

Miss Arnold[53] went over the river to Raymond to be married on Monday. Col. Manlove[54] is there. Mrs. Booth told us last week that he was over there. It is supposed that the 21st and 18th Regiments are with Johnston.

We see in the Yankee papers that the Rev. Mr. Gibson[55] has arrived in Cairo. He gives a glowing account of the Rebels and the opposite of the Feds. As he is travelling at the expense and favor of Gen. Grant, we think he is rather ungrateful than otherwise. Good for Mr. Gibson.

Mary left last night with her children. A wagon came for her. She is to cook for Osterhaus she says.

FRIDAY, JUNE 26, 1863

Mary returned with her children yesterday. Thought better of her trip but this morning some Yanks were in conversation with her so last night she stole one of Mrs. Batchelor's saddles and was off again. A Yank came for her. I am sorry, for Joe's[56] sake, that she has the children.

Yesterday I spent the day at Mrs. Noland's and heard of the romance of Miss Arnold, Mrs. Booth having given the particulars. Col. Manlove was wounded at Chancellorsville, was at home on furlough. He sent his servant across the [Big Black] river to Capt. Barnes'[57] with a note to Miss Arnold begging her to come to him and never to leave him. She was very much excited, doubtful how to act, asking Mrs. Booth's and Mrs. Barnes'[58] advice. They said go – if she ever expected to marry him go now. She took a small bundle on the horn of her saddle and set out with some other lady. The servant boy in the meantime was concealed upstairs. They did not think it safe for him to return at the same time. When she reached the other side of the river she was met by Col. Manlove, who had some sort of a buggy and horse. They drove to Raymond,[59] and were married. His family are at Brandon.[60] It is said his mother was very much opposed to the match. She [Miss Arnold] was poor and a governess.

This boy [Manlove's servant] brought the news that Breckinridge[61] was in Jackson and some other news. We hear this evening that Port Hudson has fallen, that the lower fleet is at Vicksburg. We do not believe it.

This morning before we were dressed Capt. Young sent the carriage with a guard who told us that the Yankees were coming for Capt. Young – but I forgot to say that the night before after we had retired, about a dozen men rushed into the house, surrounded the house, banged at the back door, and demanded admittance. Mr. Noland met them. They inquired for Capt. Young and Mrs. and Miss Brabston. Mr. Noland told them that Capt. Young was at Mrs. Downs and Mrs. Brabston at home, he supposed. They said Mr. Brabston wished to get through the lines and that Capt. Young had been seen in their company that evening. It was supposed he was going to escape. They mounted horses after the officer had collected his men by calling out "Attention" and rushed out of the yard frantically. Vic was sleeping downstairs, so soon as they knocked she rushed upstairs, woke me up. By the cry of "Yankees," I instinctively went to my trunk tied my sock around my waist, Vic doing the same, each taking a "contraband" in our hands, waited for an assault.[62] They in the meantime rode into Mrs. Downs yard in the same desperate manner as if (as Miss Rebecca told it) an army of Confederates were at their heels.

She and Capt. Young, with a Mr. Lewis, who is acting guard, were sitting in the parlor. Their first thoughts (as Vic said) were that they were our cavalry. They surrounded the house. The officer, who is a Lieut. Foster, one of Osterhaus' Aid de Camp, with one or two of his men went into the hall [and] demanded Capt. Young. He made his appearance. They told him their errand, asking him about Mrs. Brabston. He said he knew nothing of her, that he had merely stopped at her house a few moments to see Miss Mary before they left the lines as they had a pass to go to Jackson the next day.

"They will not go tomorrow," he said.

"And did they whip that nigger wench" was the inquiry from one of the company.

"Don't ask me," said Capt. Young. "I know nothing of the matter. Besides, I do not choose to be questioned as if I were arraigned at the Bar."

He talked to the Lieutenant and soon convinced him that he had acted foolishly, that he had had every opportunity to cross the river if he had been so inclined but that he would not break his parole for any amount. They stayed about two hours and took their leave.

A Yankee in the meantime had gone into Mrs. Downs' room, picked up her comb, and after combing his head put it into his pocket and walked out. Mrs. Downs went after the officer, who pursued the man, and the next morning it was found on the gallery.

The officer told Capt. Young that Gen. Grant had issued an order that all officers should be sent North, that they would probably come for him the next day. He sent word for the Provost to come for him, so this morning he sent us word. We went over as we had promised to do. We found them all very "blue." They had sat up nearly all of the night before, all had taken a good cry. Poor Capt. Young. He hates to be sent North and probably shot for a Negro.[63] Well, we waited all day.

We also wanted to see the Provost, as we had heard that he had recovered the silver, but no one appeared.

Miss Rebecca and Capt. Young rode home with us. Before we left a Yank whom we have demoralized came in. When he heard the news he was much distressed, said he would rather a whole regiment had been killed. We found two officers here on our return. Gen. Osterhaus passed this evening on his way to look after his pickets. Capt. Young, being very much taken with Vic, wished to remain all night but Mrs. Downs thought he had better return in case they came after him.

Mrs. Batchelor and Mrs. Noland are greatly distressed because Mr. Hal Noland and Mr. Pearce Noland have taken the Citizens' Oath, which is but a milder name for that of Allegiance. They say it is a disgrace to the name. Both Mr. Vaughn Noland and Mr. J. [Joseph Noland?] are furious. It was done sometime ago. Mr. Hal Noland was deceived when he took it. He went after rations with Billy Miller,[64] who persuaded him to do it. The Provost said it meant nothing, only a preventive of guerrillas, but Mr. Pearce Noland took it several days after, together with Mr. Thompson and McGarr,[65] had it fully explained (for Mr. Booth and Sally Newman were present) that they were not to aid or abet the Confederate Cause in any way during the war. Mr. McGarr asked if it would protect them in any way. On the contrary, they were told that it was done as a means to protect themselves.

"Are we compelled to take it?"

"No, it is a voluntary act."

We have heard that an attempt was made to blow up Fort Hill with twenty one kegs of powder, but half exploded, enough of the Fort was destroyed to enable them to plant a gun, which commanded part of [our] works, that 150 men had been killed. (Story).[66]

SATURDAY, JUNE 27, 1863

This morning before breakfast here came Mrs. Downs carriage with a note to come over immediately, as the Provost would be there, to carry off Capt. Young in a short time. We went. We found two men there guarding the house, had been sent out the night before. Capt. Young was very restless, talked about the disagreeable trip he was about to make and so on, looked sentimental at Vic, told me I must take good care of her.

He is without doubt a noble young man. He offered to remain here, even petitioned (as his place was with Price)[67] to defend Vicksburg, left his home in Missouri and now a prisoner. Perhaps his fate may be to be shot for one of these rascally negro officers.

We wanted to see the Provost as he had heard that he had recovered some of the silver. About 11 o'clock he arrived attended by the same little lieutenant who appeared very much ashamed of his conduct the evening before, said some rascal had brought the news into camp that Young was about to go out of the lines with Mrs. Brabston and Mary. We all laughed very much at him. He appeared very much annoyed, blushing very much. We told him Mrs. Brabston would feel of so much consequence.

We asked about the silver. The Provost said he had recovered some of it and would leave it at Mrs. Brien's. He would bring it out, but this was so entirely off of his road. Mrs. Downs begged them to stay to dinner, but as they wished to go to Grant had not time. At last they left. The lieutenant rode in the buggy with Capt. Young. We do not know where they will send him. A man came out in the morning from Grant with an ambulance, which he left at the picket lines with orders that Capt. Young should be brought to him. He also said that there was a whole squad of cavalry waiting to see the "Rebel Officer."

When we came home we found Mrs. Batchelor much better. This evening Anderson, Jim and Mose came home on a visit. Anderson says Mary is in camp sewing for the Provost, that Lucinda is with him, she wants to come home, he intends bringing her, says that a deserter came in from over the Big Black who gave his reason for deserting, that he had struck his captain so knew he would be shot – chose desertion. He told the Yanks that Johnston was coming, has 60,000 men, that the Confederates would contest every inch of ground [in] the South and the North could never conquer them. Anderson said the man had received the news from the North of what Lee was doing. Some cursed and swore they did not believe it, others said it was so. Col. Hammond told Mrs. Pearce Noland that there had been no official report of the taking of Port Hudson, it was only a rumor.

Mrs. Brabston and Miss Mary passed over into Jackson yesterday. Anderson says Miss Mary sent her respects to us all.

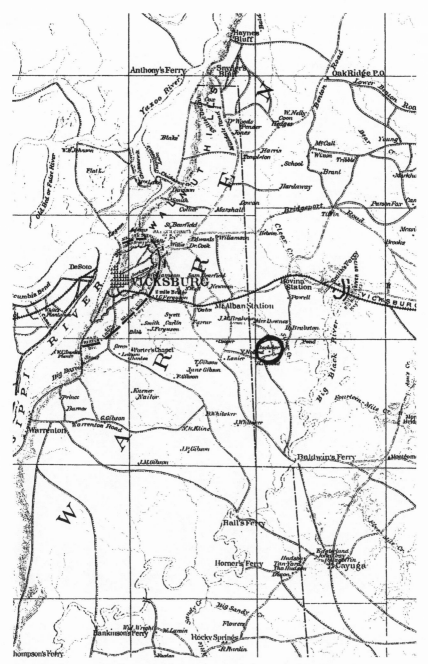

The Batchelor plantation, Hoboken, was about seven miles east of Vicksburg near the Mount Alban community and only a few miles south of the
main route taken by the armies. *Official Military Atlas of the Civil War*
(1973 edition), plate 36, map 1.

The Warren County Courthouse was a new building when this photo was taken in 1861. The lawn was not landscaped and terraced until after the war. Old Court House Museum Collection, Vicksburg, Miss.

Retreating Confederates burned the bridge over the Big Black River near Bovina, east of Vicksburg, on 17 May 1863, on their retreat into Vicksburg. Nothing remained but the pillars. Old Court House Museum Collection, Vicksburg, Miss.

Gen. James B. McPherson and his staff posed in the backyard of the Balfour House, where he had his headquarters following the siege in 1863. McPherson is seated, near the middle, wearing a Hardee hat. Old Court House Museum Collection, Vicksburg, Miss.

John C. Pemberton, the Confederate general who commanded troops at Vicksburg in 1863, was a Pennsylvanian who cast his lot with the South. Old Court House Museum Collection, Vicksburg, Miss.

Maj. Gen. U. S. Grant, commander of Union troops at Vicksburg, had this picture taken by army photographers Barr and Young in Vicksburg in 1863. Old Court House Museum Collection, Vicksburg, Miss.

Union troops built pontoon bridges across the Big Black. Following the siege, these bridges were also used by civilians. The photo was taken from the Warren County side, looking toward Hinds County, which the Yankees called "Rebeldom." Old Court House Museum Collection, Vicksburg, Miss.

Northern soldiers stole Mrs. Ellen Batchelor's silver service, which General Osterhaus managed to recover and return to her. In the early 1900s the Batchelor home burned, and this piece is all that was saved. It is on display at the Old Court House Museum in Vicksburg. Photo by Bob Pickett.

3

"Enough to Sicken the Heart"

SATURDAY, JULY 4, 1863

Report says Vicksburg has fallen, but I cannot and will not believe it. That hateful lieutenant at Mrs. Brabston's wrote Miss Rebecca a note – "Glorious fourth! Vicksburg has <u>fallen</u>. What do you think of it? Where is the illustrious Johnston? Why don't he come?" We were very indignant and wrote in answer what we thought of Hooker.[1]

We hear that Pemberton had been out to Grant last evening, had agreed to surrender it [the city] and this morning at ten o'clock they are to march in.[2]

SUNDAY, JULY 5, 1863

This morning Vic and I rode to Mrs. Brien's to get the silver Capt. Carnahan, the Provost Marshal, had promised that he would be there with, but of course he disappointed us. Mrs. Folkes who was in the parlor with Col. Hammond came out as we were about to leave, when Vic told her to tell Capt. Carnahan that she said he had treated her very ungentlemanly by not keeping his promise. She [Mrs. Folkes] immediately defended him by saying that he had started with it but Gen. Grant had issued an order that nothing should be returned. It may be so, but I do not believe it.

When we reached home we found some men here in the cellar noting down what there was there. They reported that Mrs. Batchelor had been drawing rations at different places and had also been feeding rebels across the river. About twelve o'clock some men came and arrested Mr. Noland and Mr. Webb, by order of Gen. Osterhaus. After they (Mr. Noland and Mr. Webb) had eaten dinner, they were taken off. Late in the evening about a dozen men came with two negroes for the provisions in the cellar. They cursed and ripped around, took everything except barely enough for twelve days – filled the wagons. Mr. Booth rode up in the midst.

There was a lieutenant sitting on the front gallery. A clever sort of man, he did not come with the rest. He appeared very much ashamed, went out,

looked at their order, told them to leave the coffee. They behaved shame-
fully. I never heard so much cussing. West, a negro boy who had been in
town, came up. We had heard that Dr. Batchelor had sent a note out. We
asked him for it. He said he did not have any, making an awful face at the
same time at us, on account of the Yanks. Presently, after Vic went into the
hall, he followed and gave her the note. It was written on the blank part of
a newspaper. It simply stated that he was a prisoner and expected to be sent
to Johnston. They were all to be paroled. We were all much distressed about
the provisions. Mrs. McGaughey cried, said her children would starve.

MONDAY, JULY 6, 1863

Mr. Noland and Mr. Webb returned last night at ten o'clock. They were
taken to the Bridge then to Gen. Grant. They saw Col. Rawlins[3] who dismissed them immediately, said there was no sense taking men up for nothing. These Yanks said Mr. Noland had been seen riding towards the river
and had a bucket in his hand. On negro information they had been arrested.
Mr. Noland told them of these same men taking notes of what they had in
the cellar. Col. Rawlins looked at it and was indignant – said it was prepos-
terous. What if she did have these articles in her cellar. She had a right to
have them – but they did not bring them back.

THURSDAY, JULY 7, 1863

Mrs. Batchelor and Mrs. Downs went to town today to see Dr. Batchelor.

FRIDAY, JULY 10, 1863

Vic and I went into town yesterday. It took us the whole of Wednesday
to find mules and driver. Mose as a great favor at last concluded to drive us
although he informed us he did not want to drive. Put him to anything else
he would be willing to do it, but not drive. He used to pretend that he was
very fond of it. The vanity of human life at least, is remarkable.

We started early in the morning in the carriage, drawn by two mules,
one about half the size of the other. I told Vic it was a judgement sent on
us for laughing at Mrs. Fox's poor little mules they used to drive to
Church.[4] We stopped at Mrs. Downs. They were all ready to go but had not
breakfasted.

We were about five hours getting to town. The roads near town were
blockaded. We had to drive around the fortifications. The roads of course
were bad. I thought we were [going to turn] over several times. The Yanks
have fortified beyond imagination – two or three rows of breastworks. The
Yanks at last did not take Vicksburg, but starvation [did]. The men actually
had to eat mules. Some people ate dogs. They say the mules ate very well.
Some of the men had to be lifted out of the trenches to stack their arms.
The same men stayed in the trenches seven weeks, but poor fellows, they
never complained.[5]

The Yanks were riding up and down the streets on the finest horses. Vic and I with Lt. Martin[6] went to the Court House to get permission to bring Dr. Batchelor home with us. He readily gave it, although Mrs. Folkes had the moment before tried to get him one. I knew she could do nothing.

Capt. Young got permission to stay at Mrs. Downs until his wound gets well. He through the intercession of our general is to be treated as the surrendered officers.[7]

It is horrible to think that Vicksburg is really gone. The [men] lay in the trenches the whole time, some had to be lifted out to stack their arms, and then cried because they were obliged to do it. When taking their paroles, some swore they would soon be in the field again. I hear many complain of Pemberton.[8] Some mistrust his loyalty, others say he is perfectly loyal but inefficient. The men had mules given them for rations. Some poor people ate cats and dogs. Sometimes the firing would continue all day. The rations would be given out at night.

SUNDAY, JULY 12, 1863

This morning Dr. Batchelor left for the other side of the river; he mounted a mule. He did not want to leave his home at all but preferred it to remaining in the Yankee lines. Besides, Pemberton wishes to keep his army together. We do not know where they will go – to Georgia, probably.[9]

Some old looking men passed along this morning. We gave them some butter milk. Mrs. Downs and Mrs. Brabston rode up to Dr. Newman's yesterday morning. Mrs. Booth was crying at the sight of our poor men. Gen. Pemberton and staff rode up. Mrs. Downs invited them to dinner. They accepted and went down with her. He seemed grateful for her kindness as he must hear many of the reports about him. A courier rode up with a dispatch from Grant. He read it, put it in his jacket, and ordered the courier to return. Capt. Young asked him if he was not going to answer it. He said he never answered anything they wrote him. Pemberton, they say, is a fine looking man, quiet in manner, firm eyes, taciturn and grave.

Capt. Young was kept at Chickasaw Bayou a week.[10] While he was there he met some of our couriers who had been taken. One acted the citizen to perfection. He had his dispatches in his sleeve. He pretended that he was from Tennessee and wanted to get his wife out of Vicksburg. They released him and he went on his way rejoicing to Johnston. Capt. Young says he never spent so unhappy a day as he spent on the 4th. About a thousand Yanks told him that Vicksburg was "gone up."

Dr. Coffee[11] says he amputated several limbs for ladies in town struck by shells. The town looks very little injured. It is astonishing. The Yankees refused to allow our men or officers to take their servants with them. Some of the negroes cried to come home, but it could not be.[12] They gave them freedom which they immediately take from them. Poor negroes – fate is a sad one. Dr. Batchelor was obliged to leave Isom.[13] He has not returned yet.

MONDAY, JULY 22, 1863

Rain this evening for the first time in a month. We were very thankful as the cisterns were entirely dry. I hope it will rain all night.

Vic and I want to go to Vicksburg tomorrow. Yesterday Mrs. Batchelor, Mrs. Brabston, and Mrs. Downs started to town in the carriage and Miss Rebecca and I in the buggy with a mule. Miss Rebecca drove. We had quite a time. When we got to our fortifications, we found pickets stationed. We had received passes from a surgeon. The pickets informed us that that was not sufficient.

Henry Bolls was going into town. We told him to go to Gen. McPherson and send us passes. He promised to go and send us word immediately if we could come in. We waited two hours patiently, then turned our vehicles and came home, accomplishing nothing.

A Yankee rode behind the buggy for some distance [and] gave us some candy. Miss Rebecca said rather than go back into the Union she would prefer some one to kill her, that she would kill herself.

The man said, "Well, you are the wickedest girl I ever heard talk."

We were busily talking when he pitched the candy in the buggy. "Here, gals, here is some candy for you."

Miss Mary went to the Bridge today to draw rations. She also went to see Mary again, as Mrs. Batchelor has lost her mantle and collar. Mary abused her, said she should not have the things, and as for the underclothes she had taken from her, she would burn them up, said she would rather jump into Big Black than live with Mrs. Batchelor again. She was always high-tempered.

Vic and I did the ironing today, the second we had done. Henrietta is the only servant left. All of Mrs. Noland's left yesterday morning. We heard today that they were coming back. We do all our own work now, except the cooking and washing, but we do it willingly. Agnes and Jennie milk. The other day Miss Mary was walking along when she met one of our soldiers. She said, "Are you a Rebel?"

"Yes," he said, "that's right."

A Yankee standing near said, "You told that man it was right to be a rebel, didn't you?"

In a very fierce manner Miss Mary said, "I said Washington was a Rebel, and that was right."

"No you didn't, no you didn't, you said it was right to be a rebel."

Miss Mary was mum.

Mrs. Booth asked who a certain general was when he left the Provost Marshal's room. She was informed that it was Gen. Stevenson.[14]

"Not our Gen. Stevenson,"[15] she remarked to Mrs. Newman when Gen. Sullivan[16] took it up.

"'Our' general indeed? I will teach you rebel women how to talk. I will tell you nothing is 'ours.'"

Mrs. Booth said she meant no offence but simply to make the distinction.

We hear that some of the people of Vicksburg are very anxious to take the oath. Can it be so after they endured the siege?

We saw a <u>New Orleans Era</u> yesterday on the 15th where we saw that Port Hudson had fallen, yielded to starvation. The men were paroled, the officers sent North. The Yanks also informed us that they had captured 8,000 head of cattle from Texas a few miles above Port Hudson.

The guard at Mrs. Downs saw Gen. Green fall.[17] He rashly got on the fortifications.

Some of Gen. Pemberton's staff gave Miss Rebecca a piece of Yankee flag that was put on our fortifications and taken in by our men. It has blood on it. I have a piece of it.

Gen. Pemberton said that only three or four of his men had been able to return when sent to Johnston – that Johnston sent him word five weeks before the surrender that he could render him no assistance, but to hold out ten days. He held out five weeks. Gen. Pemberton told Mrs. Downs that probably his visit would get her into trouble with the Yanks. She said she did not care if it did. He was astonished when he heard how we talked to the Yanks. One of the aids said that he was told that all of the ladies had turned Union and were receiving the attention of Federal officers. Miss Rebecca said someone deceived him.

Last Sunday evening Mrs. Batchelor received a note from Dr. Batchelor. The prisoners are on their way to Alabama. His mule was of great service to him. He wrote in such good spirits that we concluded that Johnston must be doing something.

THURSDAY, JULY 23, 1863

Mrs. Vaughn Noland's baby died this morning at 4 o'clock, six weeks old exactly. Last night she sent for some of us to go over. Vic and I had been ironing all day and were very tired. Miss Mary walked over, about 12 o'clock at night, as Alice could not be found. We had no idea the little darling was so ill. I certainly should have gone over had I known it as she was to have been my God-child and I was already much attached to her as I had more to do with her than I ever had with any other infant.

SATURDAY EVENING, JULY 25, 1863

I rode over to Mrs. Downs Thursday evening to get some flowers. I returned immediately.

A Yankee rode in at the same time, rode up to me and said, "I believe you have my horse."

I was on Alice. I said, "You are very much mistaken. This horse never belonged to anyone but a Noland. I would not be riding so old a horse if I had any other."

He said, "Well, I may be mistaken. I could tell if the saddle was off."

I told him he certainly was mistaken. He rode around the house, then out of the yard.

I took my basket of flowers and trimmings for the baby's coffin and started, when I soon arrived at Mr. Noland's. I found both Mr. and Mrs. Noland covering the little coffin with white silk, Mrs. Noland's wedding dress. A plain pine coffin made by the plantation carpenter. Mrs. Joseph Noland and I had been making the trimmings of pieces of the same silk, pinched on the edges and then quilled. I carried it with me. I took Mrs. Noland's place and Mr. Noland and I soon finished tucking the silk on, then I sewed the trimming on the edges of the lid and top of the coffin, also around the bottom. We put her in that night. I slept that night in the room with her. She was buried yesterday morning. No one was at the funeral but the family, Mrs. Downs, and Mrs. Booth. Mrs. Booth's family could only go to the grave yard, as we only have one poor horse.

These are terrible times. If a grown person was to die, they would either be buried by the charity of the Yankees or coffinless.

This morning Vic and I went to Mrs. Hawkins to breakfast, walked over and back. On our return we found Capt. Young here. He looked as nice as ever.

SUNDAY EVENING, JULY 26, 1863

Capt. Young stayed all night. Mrs. Downs came for him this morning. The first thing she told us was that Cheney and Amanda[18] were gone to the Yanks. She drove Ellen off.[19] She (Ellen) went to town and procured a house. We suppose Amanda and Cheney are staying with her. Mrs. Downs says she feels as if she had lost some of her children, she had taken so much pain with them, taught them to read and sing. I declare it is too bad. Amanda will not live long. I do not know of any two servants better taken care of than they were.

A Yankee informed us this evening that Fort Sumter[20] had fallen. Of course we do not believe it.

It is raining. (Something very surprising as it has been thundering and clouding up for the last week or two).

SATURDAY, AUG. 1, 1863

Mrs. Vaughn Noland and I went into Vicksburg this morning. We drew rations. All were very polite and kind to us. We first went to the Court House, were <u>ordered</u> to Gen. Smith's,[21] who is in Mrs. Manlove's house.[22] We were there directed to the proper office. In the meantime we concluded to go to Gen. McPherson as Mrs. Noland wished a passport for her mother to Woodville.[23] He gave it to her readily. We found him polite and affable but I imagine the ladies are continually with him, bringing their complaints, but it [is] just as little as he can do, to answer them and redress their wrongs.

THURSDAY, AUG. 4, 1863

Today Vic and I went to the Bridge to recover the best cow Mrs. Batchelor had, which the Yankees carried off on Sunday. We met Mrs. Dr. Cameron,[24] Miss Phillipps, Mrs. Bolls, and Henry Bolls. Mrs. Cameron gave some amusing accounts of her fights with the Yanks. She is just the woman to battle with them. She came to procure some medicine for her sick child, also to try and have her negroes driven off the place. She has all of her own work to do, her negroes in the meantime criticizing her – "Just see what she has come to."

Mrs. Bolls came for a guard. There were also some ladies from Hinds. One came for a mule to [use to] grind [corn], others for rations. Two ladies with one of our surgeons had come from Raymond for rations. They were allowed to return, but he was detained until some wagon trains which had been sent to Raymond for the sick had been heard from. It was supposed they had been cut off by some of our men.

We at last introduced ourselves to Gen. Dennis'[25] tent. He is quite a tall man with a pleasant face. He was really kind to us, talked and laughed with Vic. He said the young ladies were great rebels and induced the young men to go to the war. Vic told him they were patriotic enough to go without any persuasion. He said there was one circumstance he had noticed among Southern ladies he had met, and that was a great many were always bright and cheerful, even gay and lively, and that under misfortunes which could crush many people, when everything was stolen from them and they came to him, to state their wrongs, and have them righted they were hopeful and cheerful. A Northern lady under the same circumstances would hardly be able to speak for her tears.

We had been promised a guard by a Col. Hennison – Inspector Gen. on somebody's staff – so we did not make any request of that kind.

On our way back we concluded we would stop and see about our guard. The General was staying in Mrs. Cameron's house. While we were there talking who should rush out of the house but Louise.[26] She with all the rest were there waiting on the General and staff.

The guard came down this evening and already he has found work to do. His orders are very strict – nothing to be touched on the place. If they refuse to obey his orders, he must shoot them.

WEDNESDAY, AUG. 5, 1863

A crowd has already been running around this morning – took the cows, went to the mill where they were grinding and into the orchard, but the guard righted it all. These guards are a great institution.

Mrs. Downs has just heard that Mr. Gus Downs was dead. I do not believe it. They say he died on the 19th of July of billious fever. A white man brought the news. Died on Deer Creek.[27]

SUNDAY, AUG. 16, 1863

Mrs. Downs sent for me last Wednesday week. I went over and remained until Monday evening. Capt. Young is still there, also Lieut. Holmes.[28]

Last Monday morning a Confed rode into Mrs. Downs' yard. Miss

Rebecca was on the gallery. She thought at first he was a Yank. He inquired if there was a guard, said he had orders to carry off guards but would not as she was responsible for him.

Miss Rebecca said, "What are you, are you a Confederate?"

When he said he was, she said, "Oh! Ain't you afraid to be in here? The Yankees will get you."

She says he looked so independent, rode a fine horse, said he was not afraid, told her to keep her guard close. He and another captured five Yanks at the quarters. He rode out and <u>shut</u> the gate after him, convincing proof of what he was.[29]

The guard, after the Rebs left, came out of the bushes trembling like a leaf.

"Oh, if I had known they were rebels and had had my gun, I would have laid one of them on the grass."

"And yes," said Miss Rebecca, "you would soon have lain beside him."

"How, why," said the Fed.

"Why, I would have shot you myself."

He simply looked natural, that is to say foolish.

About ten o'clock we saw a bright light towards Mrs. Batchelor's. We all said it was her gin house, which it proved to be.

Some five or six Confederates had captured a wagon train of Yanks, 18 mules and 20 men – carried them off in triumph. Pretty good for six men. About an hour after another wagon train came along heavily guarded. The negroes soon posted them, one old woman inventing for the rest. The lieutenant in command came to the house to make inquiries. He was told we had nothing to do with it. He immediately went to the gin house and ordered it to be burned. They felt so much like heroes, Don Quixote fighting against wind mills. The mill for grinding is the greatest loss at present. Kezziah informed them that forty rebels had been fed the night before at the house. Some of the men made her courier immediately and dispatched her to town with a letter to that effect, but nothing has been said or done yet.

Mrs. Batchelor had gone to town that morning and Vic was at Mr. Vaughn Noland's sitting up with Mrs. Tigner, so when I arrived at home I found all looking disconsolate enough. We were very uneasy about the house. The next day Mrs. Batchelor came home declaring that she never went anywhere but there was some bad news on her return.

Tuesday evening Vic and I sat up with Mrs. Tigner. She had died that day about one o'clock. We did very well until nearly morning when I thought I should certainly go to sleep. Poor Mrs. Tigner was buried on Wednesday evening. Miss Mary went to town and bought a casket.[30] Dr. Harper borrowed the money for them. They have three bales of cotton. A sutler says he will give them $60 a bale for them. They will be obliged to dispose of them immediately as the man wants his money. If they cannot do this they must sell their silver. I declare these times are enough to sicken the heart. Our dead even cannot be buried as we would have them, and then we hear reports of influential men wishing to go back into the Union.[31] The heroic dead would rise and prevent such a monstrosity.

I told a Yankee adjutant who had been staying at Mrs. James Brabston's that I hated the Stars and Stripes, that he knew that [when] I was brought up children were taught to love and venerate the flag of the U.S. but now I hated it. He was astounded. I told him the misery it had brought into the land was unpardonable.

While all but Mrs. Batchelor were at the graveyard some Yanks came into the yard, said they wanted some milk. Mrs. Batchelor told them she did not have any.

"I expect you gave it all to the rebels."

She told them she had not seen any.

"You lie," one of them said.

They were about to dismount when an officer came and drove them all out of the yard.

Vic and Capt. Young went up in the buggy yesterday to draw rations. Had a glorious time, Capt. Young informed me. I told him I did not see how it could have been so pleasant riding in the hot sun but he was firm in persisting that he enjoyed himself.

FRIDAY, AUG. 17, 1863

This morning a Yankee captain came into the yard for water. When he went out to join his company a negro from Sligo, Monroe, told him that there were rebels down in Mr. Noland's field. The whole company filed off and galloped toward the place. We heard nothing more from them until this morning about three o'clock. The same company returned with seven Confederates. They had captured them in the swamp. One Yank told Mr. Street they never would have been able to [have] found them if Monroe had not piloted them.

We asked the Yankee captain to allow them to come into the yard. He said we might go out and see them. They got off their horses and came to us, shook hands with us, seemed very glad to see us, not at all cast down or dispirited, laughed and talked with us. One man in a blue shirt said he liked to have gotten [away] but his horse stumbled. The Yankee captain said he had chased him a mile himself. There were only seven of our men and at least fifty Yankees. One tall, nice looking fellow said he had been here a few days ago and helped take the twenty Yanks. He wanted to know if we would send a note to his captain. We said we would, but when he called the Yankee captain to obtain his permission he said he must wait until he got to the General. We gave them some water. The Yanks did not appear very well pleased to see us making such an ado over them. They were not allowed to remain five minutes but were hurried off. One poor fellow was drowned in Big Black. The Yanks said they tried to recover his body but were unable. The captain said he tried to get them to fight but could not. Very wonderful, we thought it – seven against fifty. It has made us all heart sick.

4

"They Shiver at Their Own Shadows"

MONDAY, SEPT. 7, 1863

Miss Rebecca Robinson[1] was married the 24th of last month to Lieut. Holmes.

This morning an order was received from Sherman to the effect that if any more rebels came into the county the citizens should be removed within the Confederate lines and their property destroyed. They say we harbor rebels. Mrs. Batchelor was not at home. At the time she and Mr. Street had gone to the Bridge to see Osterhaus. He was quite polite, said he did not take negro testimony in regard to the capture of his men. He also said the ladies had killed Gen. Dennis (he had been removed in wretched health). He said one day he came to see him but could not, he was surrounded by about a hundred ladies.

Gen. McPherson was just such another. Mr. Street was quite pleased with his visit, obtained a pass out of the lines. He, Capt. Young and Mr. Hal Noland leave on Thursday. I expect we will all be obliged to go before long.

WEDNESDAY, SEPT. 9, 1863

The other day Mrs. Batchelor told Gen. Osterhaus she hoped he did not intend to make war on the women and children. He replied he did not know as to that, that the women carried on this war. He had intercepted many a letter from the young ladies in which they urged their lovers to fight well and never give up. Mr. Street says he was a gentleman. Mrs. Batchelor says he thought so because the General did not knock him down.

Mrs. Batchelor, Vic and Jennie have gone today to obtain a pass for Mr. Joe Noland to go out of the lines and return. He wants to see his sister in Jackson. Vic and I want to go out in the carriage. Mrs. Batchelor says we may go but had better not. Mrs. Green is very ill.

Today while we were at dinner some Yanks rode up. Mr. Noland went out. They jumped out into the dining room and asked if all those people lived in that house.

Last Friday Willie Aldridge[2] and Mrs. Downs' guard went down on the Big Black fishing. They had not been there very long when four Confeds came up to take possession of Mr. Wade. He said he was a guard. They said he should have been at the house. They took the two guns, hid them, showing Willie where. Went up and down the river several miles on the look out for more Yanks. Willie said he wanted to go home, that his Aunt M. would scold him.

"Oh, no," one said, "Rebel ladies never scold."

They at last permitted him to go home with the injunction not to be found in bad company again. Willie came for me this next morning to go to his aunt's. I asked him if he were frightened.

"Yes," he said. "They like to have given me a chill."

Mrs. Batchelor sent her guard to camp. He was of no use as he made a daily visit with a cart to sell all he could procure.

FRIDAY, SEPT. 11, 1863

This evening Mrs. Batchelor and Mr. Noland rode over to Mrs. Downs. They had been gone about fifteen minutes when Anderson called to us that there were some Confederates on the gin house hill. We ran out on the gallery when a man rode up to the front gate and called, "I am one of Wirt Adams'[3] men. How many Yankees are there about here?"

Miss Mary and I went out to the gate. He told us that there were twenty-four of them at the gin house and more at the river. We knew nothing, consequently could give no information, much to our regret. He said he knew Isom very well. If we would send for him, we would know that he was not a Yankee in disguise. I told him I did not know how many Yanks there were but probably Isom would be able to tell him. I ran to the house; Isom was at the quarters. When he came up he recognized him as a Mr. Wolfe[4] in Capt. Barnes company. I am afraid he thought we did not wish to tell him anything when nothing would have given us greater pleasure than to have given him all the information possible.

Mr. Noland and myself were fully convinced that the house would be burnt that night. Thinking it expedient to be packing, we concluded to send for Mrs. Batchelor. She arrived quite excited but concluded it would be best to wait. That morning a squad of men under the lieutenant of the same Yankee captain who had been so unfortunate as to capture seven of our men (he is considered a very brave fellow by his men, and is now very sick) paid a short visit on the other side of the river when ten were captured and one killed. The lieutenant gave the command, "Take care of yourselves, boys" and set the example by putting spurs to his horse and devoutly praying that he might see this side of the river once more. The negroes at Sligo say two of our men were in the quarters sometime this evening and were hardly out of it when a squad of Yanks rode in.

MONDAY, SEPT. 14, 1863

Mrs. Batchelor and Mrs. Noland went to Gen. Osterhaus' headquarters yesterday, according to appointment, and obtained their services of silver. He had arrested them [the thieves] before he left the Bridge a month ago, but no one calling for [the silver, it] had remained in Vicksburg until now. They have heard that Col. Wilson has three forks and spoons. Gen. Osterhaus sent down the silver today. We were all delighted to see it again.

A regiment of Yankees under Col. Fletcher[5] are going to camp in that level place below the quarters. I am very sorry we are to see so much of the Yanks. Col. Fletcher, his major, besides several others stopped in [the] yard, dismounted and talked a while. They after while rode off in a gallop to the school house, then scampered back. Three rode to the lot where they stopped and looked around. Saturday morning a fellow came for milk, said he was a picket. He had a nice Maynard rifle captured from one of the seven [Confederates]. It had engraved on it "E. Scroggs presented by Capt. Rogers."

Mr. Vaughn Noland and myself went over to Mrs. Downs yesterday morning. Miss Rebecca was well but the lieutenant was not yet up. It was 12 o'clock.

Miss Rebecca and Mrs. Noland went to Gen. Osterhaus' headquarters Saturday to look for their cows. While they were there two of our officers came over under a flag of truce. Gen. Osterhaus introduced them to the men as "two of your very good friends." Miss Rebecca said she knew they would only be in the way and so left. Gen. Osterhaus told Mrs. Batchelor that he spent a delightful day, that one of them was the most elegant gentleman he had seen.

Some Yanks a day or two ago took possession of Mr. Pearce Noland who was on his way home after a visit to his brother. They told him he was the only citizen they had met and wanted him to accompany them. They kept him in the hot cornfield where they were gathering corn several hours. When he reached home he was quite sick.

There are some Yanks on the gallery now. I hear Ida[6] asking one of them if he is going to see the Rebel soldiers. They laughed when Carroll[7] told them he was a Rebel. He was quite indignant at the chap who called him a Yankee.

Gen. Osterhaus told Mrs. Batchelor that we all loved and venerated Washington, but Lincoln was far his superior in every respect. He was one of the greatest men the world ever produced.

TUESDAY, SEPT. 15, 1863

Yesterday evening Vic and I rode over to Mrs. Downs. We found her at home, also Lieut. Holmes. Mrs. Noland and Miss Rebecca had gone for the cows that had been taken. On our way home we passed some pickets but they did not notice us. Isom went over to Greenbrier[8] for Mrs. Vaughn Noland's carriage. On his way back he was stopped by the pickets. They would not allow him to pass but carried him to Col. Fletcher who said they had no right to stop them. He called this morning and said he had given orders that we should not be stopped.

He will make his headquarters at Sligo.

Mrs. Noland got back her guitar that a Yank had stolen.

There are pickets at the school house.

There was a Yank here yesterday, a deserter from Price's army.[9] He said he was living with a Secesh lady at the time the war broke out. She persuaded him to join the rebel army. He was afterward convinced of his errors and joined old Lincoln.

We heard yesterday that there had been a fight at Hall's Ferry[10] – cavalry fight – we whipped the Yanks all to pieces. Five miles strewn with the dead.

FRIDAY, SEPT. 18, 1863

Wednesday morning a Yankee came into the yard for milk. Seeing Miss Mary, who was sweeping off the back gallery, called out, "Halloo, old lady, give me a biscuit."

She indignantly replied, "Thank you, I am not an old lady."

Hannah,[11] who was standing, said "Why, she is a right young lady."

The fellow shrugged his shoulders.

That same morning there were three men here. One said he had sisters and brothers living in Montgomery, Ala. He supposed they were rebels, if so he would like to kill them. He heard Jennie practicing but I had given her instructions to lock the door and shut the blinds that they might not be able to get in. He had nearly reached the parlor door when he concluded that they had locked themselves in.

Wednesday morning Jennie and I walked over to Vaughn Noland's. The carriage followed, loaded. Mrs. Batchelor had been to town the day before, had seen a number of people. Mrs. Montgomery[12] had gotten her son off. The eldest had been taken prisoner and made his escape. Her guerrilla son said they would never take him again under a bed. She also met a lady from Jefferson [County]. She brought news that a gunboat had been taken and several officers made prisoners.[13]

I remained at Sligo all night. Mr. Booth rode over on Thursday morning. He gave us a description of Pattie's[14] first interview with the Yanks. They searched the house for arms. She was very indignant and told one if she had a pistol she would shoot him.

"Well, here is one," he said, at the same time handing her one.

"Oh, I don't want it," she said, starting back, proving that her will was good but not her courage.

There are two regiments camped around the yard, on the black people's grave yard hill, pickets between here and the school house, also at the cow pen. It really looks as if we were guarded.

Col. Fletcher of the 31st Missouri is the most gentlemanly man I have yet seen in the Federal Army. He and several other officers were here this evening. He called to tell Mrs. Batchelor that if any of his men annoyed her, in any way, he would like to know of it. We have the extreme pleasure of hearing the drum and bugle for morning and evening roll, etc.

Yesterday evening on my return home from Mrs. Vaughn Noland's, when I arrived at the pickets, lo! and behold I was stopped. My indignation was unbounded. They appeared very sorry, sent one of the members for the lieutenant who soon came, was more sorry than his men, but his orders were very positive, no one was to pass. They would send to the colonel. I almost cried I was so angry, but having learned how more than useless it is to persuade a Yankee, I sat on my mule very patiently. Presently Lieut. Holmes and Mr. Hal Noland rode up but they had a pass but concluded to wait for me. At last the lieutenant told they might as well allow one of their men to go with me home. They concluded to do so.

I descended from my mule and gave it to my escort, in the shape of an "unbleached American," and gave him his orders to hurry home. I was afraid they would not allow him to return. When I reached the house I found three officers seated up in the parlor. My blood rose immediately to fever heat again. At the supper table we all had quite a war of words. They were speaking and laughing about the carriages they had stolen. One fellow said, well, the fact was they used a great many carriages for ambulances. Half of the army was riding. I told him I thought more than half were riding now.

He flashed his eyes at me, across the table. "I hope you do not like to hear of any human person being sick."

I said, "Of course not."

Last night a week ago a party of Yanks broke into the dairy and stole every particle of milk.

Col. Fletcher is looking for his wife by the next packet.

SATURDAY, SEPT. 19, 1863

Yesterday evening Palmer and Bowers[15] called to see us, appeared delighted at meeting us again. It seems strange how much we have demoralized those fellows.

Dr. Newlin, a Yankee surgeon, came with his instruments and chloroform to pull Vic's tooth. She would not allow it to be done until the trial had been made on Isom. When she found that it produced no ill effect she took her seat. It was some time before the chloroform had any effect but at last she fell asleep and he extracted it. Dr. Newlin stayed all night tonight.

Just before tea a Capt. Hill called to see him. He was the most pompous poor f____l I ever met with. After tea we went into the parlor. Miss Mary and Capt. Hill got into a discussion and of all the long talkers he exceeded. He laughed precisely like an owl. He said we might remember his words, that they would certainly come to pass: in a year's time this rebellion would be crushed and the Union restored. We laughed at the idea. He said he never prophesied, but that his prophecy is coming to pass.

Vic remarked, "You must be a prophet."

"No."

"Well, certainly the son of a prophet then."

"No, not the son of a prophet."

He and I had a misunderstanding and nearly approached to blows.

MONDAY, SEPT. 21, 1863

Last night there was quite an excitement in camp by a report that the Rebels were approaching. No drums were beat nor bugles sounded. 800 cavalry came from the bridge to oppose them. About 8 o'clock a gun was heard at [the] most distant picket post, then another and another. We have since heard that the whole camp was drawn into line of battle. The colonel came down to see us after the excitement was over and said the shooting was caused by some of the cavalry who came down here without anything to eat and were obliged to procure some beeves.

After we had retired an alarm was given that somebody was breaking into the dairy but it proved to be Alice and her colt. When they passed the table [they] pushed it against the dairy.

On Saturday morning before breakfast Vic and I rode over to Mr. Vaughn Noland's to carry some letters, as they were going out of the lines. The pickets at first refused to allow us to pass, but we promised to return in half an hour. We accomplished our errand in that time and returned.

Alice Hawkins invited us over to dine with her on the turkey and duck that some Yankees had shot the day before in their yard, but which Capt. House,[16] on being appealed to, obliged them to return.

While we were there Gen. Wood,[17] Colonels Fletcher, Williamson,[18] besides several others, called. They had been to Mrs. Downs' that morning. While they were there, they were speaking of Gen. Dennis' visit down here and were laughing at his fear of the rebels, so that he could hardly enjoy his visit. In the midst of their telling this joke to Mrs. Downs the picket they had stationed somewhere gave the alarm. They sprang to their feet, rushed out knocking over the chairs and everything else in their way. When they found that there was nothing to fear they returned, begged Mrs. Downs' pardon, examined the furniture to convince themselves that nothing was broken and made their adieu. So I think the joke has been turned on themselves. They shiver at their own shadows. I never saw anything like it. The Colonel told us that seven or eight rebs had been seen down on the river Sunday morning.

TUESDAY, SEPT. 22, 1863

Late yesterday evening we heard that the cows had been carried off. Our guard with Mr. Noland went up to the Colonel, who immediately went in pursuit. He found the men who had them but they said that only one of the cows had been shot. The others had returned to the swamp. This morning three came up. The original number was five.

When Mr. Noland returned he told us that part of the cavalry had returned. Capt. House had made a raid and captured a captain and his two lieutenants who were fast asleep in bed. Col. Fletcher told Mr. Noland that he thought there had been a fight on the other side of the river. He also said he had a very disagreeable duty to perform today, to remove Lieut. Holmes into the Confederate lines.

While we were at dinner today an order came for our guard to bring his things and come to camp. We do not know the why and wherefores yet.

On Sunday Mrs. James Brabston went to Sherman's headquarters to get permission to go visit her husband and bring him home. When she reached the camp accompanied by a Dr. Joyceline[19] whose wife had been sick at Mrs. Brabston's they found that the General had gone to town, was expected any time. She thought in the meantime she would pay a visit to Mrs. Sherman's tent. She found her with one of her children very ill with temp.[20] Mrs. Sherman received her very coolly – did not know when the General would return. He soon after arrived, did not ride directly to his wife's tent but to some other one. Mrs. Sherman sent one of her children who was present to tell their father that a lady wished to see him. He came in with a very red face and coarse manner, took a drink, a preliminary. Mrs. Brabston stated her errand, that she wished to see Mr. Brabston. He said he did not believe it, that the ladies around here had told him more lies. They would pretend they wanted medicine for their sick families and go straight and give it to the Rebels. Said she could not go. She must make up her mind to stay on one side or the other of the river.

She remained all night. The next morning she had another interview. Gen. Sherman was rather more polite but still unwilling for her to go. Dr. Joyceline had to go her security in writing that she meant no harm, that she only wished to see her husband and that he would be answerable if any harm came from it. Under the circumstances His Majesty concluded to let her go.

MONDAY, SEPT. 23, 1863

I have been having chills for the last week, consequently have not written.

Last week Mrs. Batchelor went to see Old Osterhaus. While she was there she saw a woman from the other side of the river. As Osterhaus and his division were about to leave, on their way up the river, and a new set to take their place, she (the other woman) wished to be introduced to some of the newcomers. She was introduced around as "Mrs. Davis, a good Union lady." He could not do the same for Mrs. Batchelor as she was known to [be] a full rebel.

In the course of the morning Col. Williamson and Mrs. Batchelor discoursed on the subject of cotton. She told him how much she had lost in the last year.

"Why, Madam, you have lost $100,000 worth. Mr. Moss[21] has recovered most of his cotton. Could you not take the oath for $100,000?"

When he heard her decided "No," he looked at her in amazement.

"Well," he said, "I believe you people are honest in what you propose, but your leaders are the most designing rascals."

She of course begged leave to differ.

We hear that all of their men have gone up the river to reinforce Rosecrans,[22] who has been badly whipped in Tennessee. Bragg[23] had taken 14,000 prisoners and 150 pieces of cannon.

This morning about 8 o'clock six Confederates rode up to the yard, two rode up to the door. One was the Mr. Rossman[24] who was here last winter on a visit. They inquired about the Yanks. They then went to Sligo. Very soon afterwards a squad of about twenty Yanks rode in that direction but in a very short time returned. They were afraid to venture any further.

WEDNESDAY, SEPT. 30, 1863

We have heard this morning that France has certainly recognized us. Mason[25] is in Mobile. The whole city was illuminated for his reception.

Rosecrans' army is completely demoralized since its great defeat.

Mrs. Batchelor and Miss Mary went to see Mrs. Brien last Monday. Mrs. Green is at home and rather better in health. Her little boy is a complete Yankee. A day or two ago, he said, "Mother, I would be sorry to kill you and grandmother and all my other relations, but if it is necessary we must do it. This rebellion must be crushed at all hazards."

Mrs. Folkes had a good deal news. She says she was bribed by a Confederate for her to deliver Colonels Fletcher [and] Jacobinson[26] into their hands. She was to bring them down here on a certain night. The Confeds were to take possession. She said she refused because she was afraid of the consequences to Mrs. Batchelor's house. She says Jacobinson says I am a great rebel. We have seen no more Confederates.

Raining all day long.

FRIDAY, OCT. 2, 1863

Gen. Grant told Mrs. Holmes when she went to see him in order to get a pass to go to New Orleans with her lieutenant that it was not safe, that ten or twelve boats had been burned.[27] Some scouts would get on at Memphis or somewhere else, when in the route would set fire to the boat and then make their escape.

SATURDAY, OCT. 3, 1863

Mrs. Batchelor and Mrs. Downs went into town yesterday. Could not see Gen. Grant. They would not allow anyone to draw rations, said Gen. Grant had issued an order that they were to be stopped. We think they will take revenge on the citizens on account of their boats being burnt.[28]

SUNDAY, OCT. 4, 1863

Mr. and Mrs. Booth were here yesterday. They gave us an account of their recent trouble when Mr. Booth accidentally met those Confederates in the Sligo quarters. Some of the negroes immediately mounted mules and rode to town to inform on him. A cavalry company came out that night and surrounded the house. They burned the pickets around the house, took corn and hay, and everything they could lay their hands on. When Mrs. Booth went to town, she went to see Gen. Grant to be remunerated. He wrote a note to this captain and sent by Mrs. Booth to him. He was furious. "What did you do that for" but he promised to return the corn and hay.

Yesterday as Vic and I were going over to Mrs. Downs, we met three Yankee officers. They wished to know the way to Bovina. They said they had just come from there in another direction. Well, we told them that the road on which they were was the right road to Bovina. When we reached Mrs. Downs we found that they had just been there. One of them, a Dutchman, insisted on having some milk. When he was told they did not have it, he went around to the kitchen and soon appeared with three glasses of milk.

One of the other said, "Why, you got the milk."

"Yes, but I had to have the cows milked first."

They heard that William[29] had an old gun in one of the negro houses. They broke the house open, took the gun, which the negro had to shoot an owl with, and broke it. They said they were regular Jayhawkers, stationed at the Bridge. They wanted to know if Mrs. Downs had seen any rebels.

"No," she told them.

"Well, have you been harboring any."

She said she did not have the pleasure of seeing any, much less harboring them.

We rode with Mrs. Down to Mrs. Brabston's. She returned from town while we were there. She says the Yankees are down, rumors of a defeat in Virginia has reached them, Meade being whipped by Lee, also the army in Louisiana annihilated, this all coming so soon after Bragg's glorious victory over Rosecrans, is sufficient for the whole Yankee nation to be thrown into a fit of the Blues. The <u>Chicago</u> <u>Times</u> gives a lengthy description of the fight in which he acknowledges they were beaten.

Mrs. Batchelor has gone to town to buy provisions (rations being stopped) as we expect to be cut off from Vicksburg before long. They intend drawing the lines so they may not be troubled with us now that they refuse to feed us.

Everybody is anxious to get paid for the cotton taken from them. Mrs. Batchelor had fifty bales taken by Osterhaus for fortifications. The other day she went to see Gen. Grant, either to get back the cotton or paid for it. We are anxious to remain but cannot if we have nothing to eat. He saw her, said Osterhaus must have used a great deal of cotton on his fortifications, that he would rather fight fifty battles than to transact this business about cotton. (They say he is a regular woman hater.) He looked annoyed and worried, walked with crutches, told her he would telegraph to Bovina to see if there was any cotton there, to return in about two hours. When she returned he said he had heard that there was a good deal of cotton. He thought it probable she might have her fifty bales.

Asked if she had sons, "Yes."

"In the army?"

"Yes, two there."

Tuesday she and Mrs. Downs have gone in to see about it, also to buy provisions.

THURSDAY, OCT. 8, 1863

Mrs. Batchelor returned from town later yesterday evening, went to see Grant, who was at dinner. Whilst she [was] waiting for him she sat in a room with six or eight officers. One of them was reading a <u>Memphis</u> <u>Appeal</u> aloud. All were listening with the most rapt attention, without a comment. They read that Charleston was impregnable and the Yankees could never take it. The Yankees this and the Yankees that, they read. One officer glanced at Mrs. Batchelor, who was laughing. She heard him whisper to one of the others, "Give that paper to that lady," but she did not get it. Presently Gen. Grant came in. She inquired about the cotton. He told her if there was any [it was] at Bovina, so today she rode there but found none.

Yesterday Col. Wilson gave her a permit to buy provisions. She could buy but a certain amount at a time. She again heard that Lee had certainly whipped Meade, a glorious victory. The Yankees were very polite on the strength of it. When they are victorious they are domineering, but when they are whipped they are humble.

When Mrs. Batchelor stopped at Mrs. Downs on her way home, she found the household on the back gallery, talking to two fellows dressed as Confederates. They were on fine horses, had a Yankee on a mule in company with them. They said they had captured him. Mrs. Downs did not believe from their actions that they were any of our men. One of them had a bottle of whiskey and was somewhat intoxicated. They asked Mrs. Batchelor if she had been to town, and what was the news. She told them of Lee's victory.

"Well, I am glad of it," one of them exclaimed, and all rode off. They wanted something to eat. Mrs. Downs told them she had nothing, and "if I were to give you anything, this Yankee would be off in a twinkle and say I was feeding a yard full of rebels."

When Mr. Noland heard it he said, "Of course they were not rebels. In the first place our men do not wear a cloth uniform,[30] and officers do not scout."

They went on to Mrs. Brabston's and behaved so badly that she was obliged to send off for some cavalry to come and take them away. They told her before leaving that they were Yanks – not necessary as she knew that from their actions.

Some Confederates made a raid somewhere around Bovina and burnt a good deal of cotton.

"The Iron Heel of Despotism"

THURSDAY, NOV. 10, 1863

October 17 Vic B. and myself left Hoboken to pay a short visit into Hinds and Madison counties. We had a pass from Gen. McPherson to report ourselves at the Bridge. When we arrived there we found Gen. Mower[1] absent. He was on a visit to the division general, Gen. Tuttle.[2] We waited for him for about three hours. He rode up about two o'clock, gave us our pass, and we left, crossed the pontoon bridge over Big Black River and went on our way rejoicing.

We passed over what had once been a beautiful country, now laid waste, and the most desolate looking region imaginable. It was enough to make our hearts ache to see the tall chimneys alone standing of what had been happy homesteads. How many pleasant conversations had been carried on around those deserted hearths by those who are now unfortunate refugees without a home to call their own, we thought from the very few houses left standing by the vandals.

At last we reached the house of a Mr. Robinson. It was quite dark. We stopped, made Isom halloo, presently an old lady came out, together with two young girls, two boys, some servants, and some dogs. We asked if we could stay the night. She at first refused, said she had nowhere for us to sleep, nothing for our mules to eat. We told her we had provisions both for ourselves and team. She at last invited us to get out and walk into the house. She took us into her only habitable room, which had several beds besides a piano, tables and chairs innumerable in it. Her husband had run his negroes off to Alabama. She was alone with her granddaughters. When the Yankees passed her house she was entirely alone. They treated her very badly. She had packed her furniture up in two rooms. When they came in the house, she shut herself up in her room. In her language she said, "They fetched things and flung open the door" at her.

We met two of Logan's[3] scouts there. We talked to them all the evening before. They seemed interested in our descriptions of what the Yankees did and said.

After we had crossed the bridge that evening and had gone about five miles we saw some Yanks sitting on the roadside fixing their guns. They were evidently in ambush. After we had gone about a mile or two farther, we met some of our scouts, Texans. They asked us if we had seen any Yanks. We told them of those we had seen but told them not to go in there as they were in ambush, but they said they would have a pop at them. About a half hour afterward here came three of them dashing back, one without a hat. They said they had run into the Yankees before they knew it. They thought two of their number had been taken. The Yanks chased them. This one had his hat shot off.

Sunday morning we took breakfast in Brownsville,[4] and enjoyed it very much. As we had nothing warm to eat since we left home the morning before, we had some nice coffee and the nicest butter cakes, some veal and corn bread. We heard then that Wirt Adams' Cavalry was only a few miles distant – and as Vic was in pursuit of her brothers, we started in that direction. We each brought out two shirts fastened around our waists and a bundle of newspapers. When we reached camp we heard that both of her brothers were at Brandon. Gen. Adams sent them word to meet us in Clinton.[5] We reached Clinton Sunday evening. The next morning they both, together with Mr. Noland, rode into town. That evening we all went out to Mr. John Robinson's, seventeen miles distant. It poured down rain before we reached the end of our journey and even hailed. It was very dark. We drove over very bad roads. Mr. Robinson was not at home so we had the house to ourselves. We remained there all day Tuesday.

Wednesday morning we started for Canton and Sharon.[6] At Canton I met Ida,[7] spent Thursday night with her. Friday morning I met Vic at Canton (she had gone to Sharon) and we journeyed back to Mr. Robinson's where we found Dr. Robinson waiting for us.

We heard in Canton that the Yankees had crossed with a large force, both cavalry and infantry, but we determined to keep on. We were not afraid of Yankees. That night at Mr. Robinson's we heard firing. Reports came that the Yankees were only five miles off where our cavalry were contesting a crossroad with them. The next morning by daylight we were awakened. After dressing very hurriedly we were told it was absolutely necessary for us to return to Canton and probably Sharon, and to keep falling back if necessary.

We opposed this order with all our powers of persuasion and eloquence with which we were gifted. We argued that we were not afraid, that the carriage wheels might be taken off and the mules run into the swamp; of no avail – back we had to go. Dr. Batchelor remained to rejoin his command.

We started off without our breakfast and reached the road just in time to keep in front of our cavalry who were retreating to Canton.

Just before reaching Canton we met Generals Loring,[8] Buford,[9] and

Featherston.[10] We also met Buford's Brigade and Adam's Brigade (Tilgh-man's old Brigade). They were on their way to meet the Yankees, had marched from Brandon that morning, but the Yankees instead of meeting them turned and fled, burning and destroying everything in their way. Our Cavalry pursued them but they would not fight, fled with great precipita-tion towards the river, did not take time to stop in Clinton, only stopping at every house on the way to rob and plunder so that many poor families in Hinds have not a blanket or comfort to keep them from freezing. Every gin house was burned far and near, so that we found many smoking on our way home the following week, besides many houses. It is said that they fairly flew over the road, only stopping to steal.

We were absent two weeks and were both glad and sorry to return. I found two letters awaiting me, both containing sad news – my dear Sis's death, and Joe's. Joe had been dead twenty months; Sis died on the 12th of September, 1863.[11]

The next week I spent at Mrs. Downs. She was quite sick. She has given me a beautiful pin set with pearls.

On Monday the 2nd Mrs. Batchelor and Jennie went into Madison [County]. They have not yet returned.

Last night some Yankee negroes with a white man went into the quar-ters to press negroes into their cavalry. Most of the men got out of their houses and hid. One man succeeded in getting out but they shot him three times, once in the hip, hand, and ear. He suffered a good deal last night. His wife begged them not to shoot, but they paid no attention to her.

It is rumored among the Yanks in Vicksburg that Bragg has whipped Thomas,[12] who has succeeded Rosecrans after his defeat at Chickamauga.

I received letters from Mr. Nichols and Mr. Washington yesterday.[13]

THURSDAY, NOV. 12, 1863

Mrs. Batchelor and Jennie returned yesterday from "Dixie." Vic spent the day with Mrs. Downs. Mrs. Annie Noland on Monday had gone across the river. She met several of our scouts. In the course of conversation, they asked her if she knew Miss Batchelor. They said they had a piece which they had cut out of a Yankee paper about her. They gave it to her after much per-suasion as they said they wished to show it to her brothers, who were in their regiment. As we have but one copy I will copy it. Written by Col. Peck-ham[14] who was camped near here for two weeks:

"My own regiment, and the 31st (Col. Tom Fletcher) are encamped about eight miles from the railroad crossing of [Big] Black river, near Baldwin's Ferry. We are on a summit of a very high hill, from which we can look over all creation. Nearby us is a family named Batchelor. There is the Widow Batchelor and Miss Vic Batchelor and three other little Misses Batchelor, and baby Batchelor and Widow Nugent and a Mr. Nugent,[15] brother-in-law to the last and uncle and brother to the others. Miss Vic has two daguerreotypes of men whom she calls her brothers, one of whom she says, 'has been in all the glorious battles in Virginia.' Vic is a stubborn traitor – draws rations and laughs at us for 'giving them to such a spirited rebel,' – declares she will fight against us when her brothers cease fighting and thinks (at least she says she does) that Yankeedom is gone up. Vic is 18, and by no means pretty, but her people think so, and are happy in her accomplishments. She can sing and play and do worsted work and use her tongue very glibly; and she is peculiar in the employment of sarcasm and thorough enumerator of hate. Fletcher, Captain Reed and I went there last night. Vic sat in the middle of the room and carried on a conversation, and her people gazed at her with utmost admiration, laughing heartily at her every denunciation of Yankees. She seemed to enjoy it herself, too, and was so extremely polite in abusing us, so courteous and willing to favor us with music and songs (such as 'The Bonnie Blue Flag,' 'All Quiet Along the Potomac Tonight,' and 'The Red, White, and Red.'), so anxious that we should stay, so anxious also that we should call again, that we could not get angry at her, and we didn't. We, too, sang or attempted to sing, 'John Brown,' 'The Union Forever,' 'Red, White, and Blue,' 'Yankee Doodle,' and 'Old Massa Run, Ha! Ha!' Vic is a fair specimen of a she rebel. She laughed sarcastically when she spoke of going to Mobile and insinuated that when we got there she would just like to see how we should look, just for the fun of it, although she abhorred suffering, even in a foe. She didn't doubt but 'from the present light we enjoyn on the subject, we really thought we would go into Mobile and where ignorance is bliss 'twere folly to be nice.' I told her that the light by which we were reading our history now was the light of victory, and were indeed happy in our ignorance of any other. Vic laughed, as much as to say, 'You'll be fooled at Mobile,' and Tom and I laughed, as much as to say we wouldn't be fooled at Mobile. So we counted ourselves even with Vic. And here we are giving rations to such people as these, who openly denounce and abuse us, who laugh at our charity at the same time they demand it, and whose male kindred are all in the armies in our front.'

Poor silly Peckham. He forgets that he and others of his kind stole everything eatable on the place before they camped around us and when they did that they shot all the cows they could lay their hands on. And some of their men even caused a stampede one night. The brave Colonels thought the Rebels must be coming.

WEDNESDAY, JAN. 6, 1864
Another year has commenced, yet no prospects of this war being brought to a close. We have read the messages of both President Davis and Lincoln, that of the first ably written, that of the other ridiculous. I was at Mrs. Downs when I heard President Davis' message read. I could but wonder at the time how any young man could hear it and not feel obliged to go

and fight now in his country's greatest need, and yet how many will sit quietly down, <u>waiting</u> for something to be done.

We spent quite a pleasant Christmas Day. Had an egg nog and cake, made ambrosia for dinner. While in the midst of it Willie Aldridge rode up, ran into the dining room and cried out "Christmas Gift!" He brought me over a nice present from Miss Rebecca, a knit cape and several other articles.

About twelve o'clock two Yankees rode up, came into the house. One was a contemptible New Yorker, an abolitionist. He talked and talked. We thought he would never go. There was a fellow with him who seemed to take delight in giving examples where the Federals had acted cruelly. He in return told many incidents where Northerners before this war had been treated badly on coming South, gave an account of a lady being tarred and feathered in Georgia and all such ridiculous things. He said he could not understand how a Northerner could sympathize with the South in "this rebellion." I told him I both had done so and did now. He was anxious to sing "John Brown" for our benefit but we gave him no encouragement to do so, though curious to hear it.

In the evening Jennie, Agnes, Emilie and myself walked over to Mrs. Bolls to a supper, came home in the evening.

Old Mr. Fox[16] on Christmas day preached in the church at Vicksburg, having first asked permission of Gen. McPherson to omit the prayer for the President, but received for his answer that he had no authority to alter anything in the Prayer Book. Mr. Fox instead of returning home thought (I suppose) that he would hold services. When he came to that prayer he offered the petition for the "President of the U.S. and all others in authority" including, of course, Beast Butler, Seward, Chase, and all others. Five ladies present could not with their own consent offer prayers for their welfare, so arose and left the church. Gen. McArthur[17] and others were present. He said the ladies must suffer for their freedom of action. Gen. McPherson must notice it, or <u>he</u> would leave the city. Accordingly there were circulars issued banishing from the city in forty-eight (48) hours Misses Ella and Kate Barnett, Ellen Martin, Laura Latham, and Mrs. Moore, for showing disrespect of the President, and whereas in future by word or action should [anyone] be guilty of disrespect to said President, should be fined, banished or imprisoned, according to the offence.

This was posted on the corners of the streets. It was hinted that if they would make suitable apologies they would be pardoned. They would not stoop to this. They went out to the Bridge on the cars, then took ambulances. Lieut. Holmes, who went up to see his brother off, said they were a merry party, said they never traveled under more favorable circumstances, though it was pouring down rain all the time. It is said Gen. McPherson was much opposed to sending them out but rather obligated to do it. It has been rumored that he is to be removed on account of his leniency, Logan to take his place.[18]

We hear that Grant has fallen back to Nashville, Bragg has been superceded by Johnston, but he (Bragg) was too good a patriot to resign and go home, but offered his services to Johnston as a staff officer. We hear from Dixie that Foote[19] proposed to make Gen. Lee Military Dictator.

Vic and Pattie are still in Madison. We do not know when to look for them back.

FRIDAY, JAN. 22, 1864

This morning two men, fresh importations from Illinois, came to see if they could lease this place. They have never been south before – asked a great many questions. It was evident they expected to make a fortune in one year. They said the negro men were to be paid $26.00 a month, the minimum $20, out of which was to be deducted their food and clothes, and any day's absence, so at the end of the year the poor negro's expenses will be greater than his wages.

They do not know the negro yet. They said they had met a "colored" man in the quarters and asked him if they would remain and work if they hired them and not run off just as they most needed them for the crops. The colored individual answered, "Oh, no, this is my home, we will not leave." The poor unsophisticated cotton planters believed themselves persuaded that they always spoke the truth at all times and places. The whole North seems crazy on the subject of planting cotton. It will be fine fun in the spring when the poor Yanks look over their fields covered with cotton blooms one day, the next to find them destroyed by the Confederates.

We hear daily that the Federals expect to make a raid into Hinds and Madison very soon.

Vic and Pattie have not yet returned. We have heard that they were expected at Mrs. Dameron's.[20]

A most ridiculous scene took place at old Mr. Townsend's[21] place about Christmas. A Yankee who had been courting a negro girl for some time concluded to be married. They were joined, therefore, by one of the colored brethering for "better or worse." The negro girl told her friends that she did not want to marry the man, but he kept after her so much she married him to get rid of him. A beautiful state of society we are living in. The favorite doctrine of Amalgamation of Beecher's[22] is about to come into fashion.

Lieut. Holmes and Miss Rebecca are living with Mr. James Brabston. I cannot understand why he is allowed to remain in these lines. The negroes at Mrs. Brabston's curse him to his face, it is said, and think nothing of fights among themselves, fire off pistols at each other, and other such innocent amusements.

TUESDAY, JAN. 26, 1864

Mrs. Annie Noland went into Madison today.

FRIDAY, JAN. 29, 1864

About ten days ago Mrs. David Gibson[23] wrote a letter to some in Hinds to send out a young lady going out into that county. She had written to tell some of the Confederates when on some raid into the county to come and take out several of her negroes who were giving her a great deal of trouble. She had applied to the Yankees several times to have them removed, but no attention had been paid to her. But after having written her letter she concluded to erase the part about the negroes, took a pencil and scratched it out. When she gave the letter to the young lady she told her there was nothing in it and were it necessary she might give it up. Consequently when at the Bridge letters were asked for, she foolishly handed this one over. Gen. Force[24] in command there, not satisfied with reading it, must take a piece of India rubber, rub out the pencil marks and read what was under it, carried it to town. Gen. McPherson accused Mrs. Gibson of writing it and ordered her out of the county (she was in town that day). On the road home she heard that pickets had been stationed near her house. She therefore to avoid them went to Capt. Barnes' and remained all night, two wagons being sent to her house in the meantime by Gen. McPherson to move her to the other side, put her down in the swamp.

The next day Mrs. Barnes went into town to see the General. She represented to him that Mrs. Gibson intended no harm in the world and promised to stand security for her future conduct. He at last consented to allow her to stay, although at her own home, and he knew she had no place to go in the Confederacy. She said if he insisted on sending her out he would be conferring a blessing to shoot her and her children.

Poor woman, she has a great deal of trouble. She lost her oldest daughter, who was grown, a few weeks ago. This almost deprived her of her reason. And then when she was cruelly ordered to leave her own home and her only shelter in the world, with several helpless children to support, is beyond belief, and for no reason in the world.

We are indeed an oppressed people. The iron heel of despotism is felt deeply.

Two Yankees were here this morning. One of them asked if Mrs. Gibson had left the lines yet. We told him no. He said he was one of the men with a wagon who sent after her. He said it was a fortunate thing for her that she did not reach home that night as they would have been obliged to have taken her across the river as they were strictly ordered to do. I would have been ashamed to have acknowledged that I had been one of the number who went to that poor woman's house that night as the ruffians completely robbed her, stole every blanket [and] towel in the house, besides the few remaining chickens she had, and destroyed everything they could lay their hands on, took all of her little son's clothes except the suit he wore, took her daughter's clothes, and to add yet greater sorrow to her heart, stole the picture she had of her dead daughter.

Now is this not more than human nature can stand? Can anyone imagine her feelings that night, away from home, when she knew her two poor little children were there alone, and those wretches desecrating the place, but much worse they must have been when she went home and found what they had been doing.

We find great difficulty in bringing anything out of town now without taking the oath. Mrs. Batchelor went in today after something to eat and the box we sent north for has arrived. She will bring it with her.

TUESDAY, FEB. 2, 1864

We were reading the Chicago Times last night and were much amused at an editorial on the number three. After mentioning the important part it has always taken in human events – as the Trinity, the Triumvirate in government, the three days of grace in the commercial world, etc. – it says this number still influences the abolition congress, the platform of all their deliberations has been a Tripartite compound whose elements are the Oath, Whiskey, and the Nigger. "These triplets require all the time and running of Congress. Now that wet nurse, Mrs. Nancy Arnold[25] nurses the Niggers, and the others join in a general hush-a-by-baby during the operation. Anon, Nurse Hale[26] trots the Oath upon his knee; and again somebody spanks or lullabys the other members of this hysterium parturition. From day to day, month to month, this trinity rules. When they are not discussing the Oath or Whiskey, they are sure to be engaged in the care of the Nigger; and if the Nigger be for a moment dropped, the subject immediately up is either the Oath or Whiskey."

They are still discussing the exchange of prisoners. Beast Butler[27] is the person appointed by the U.S. government for the exchange, but President Davis will not recognize him as a person proper for this. In the meantime our poor men are languishing in prison. And now Gen. Butler's last order is that no sympathy is to be shown them by the ladies of Maryland. Hither their kindness has partly alleviated their sufferings, but now they are to be deprived of even this. He has deservedly earned the name of Beast.

Sunday I spent the day with Mrs. Downs. About 11 o'clock a Yankee by the name of Billy Adolphus walked in. He has been in the habit of borrowing books and not returning them, but yesterday he returned them. He is one of the most disagreeable persons I have ever met. He brought a Harper's Weekly in which was a sketch of the interior of the Ladies Cabin of a boat with a shell bursting through the top. The men and women are flying in all directions. One man has fallen down on the floor. We all laughed when we saw it. Billy thought it very inhuman in us as well as the shell. He said it was not civilized to fire into transports where ladies and children were. I said they had no business on the boats. He insisted on making himself disagreeable. We changed the subject time and time again but he would dispute on every one of them.

SUNDAY, FEB. 14, 1864

I have been spending the week with Mrs. Downs, who is alone. Have not been teaching but will commence tomorrow.

We heard the first this morning that the Yankees had some of our men at the Bridge in irons. They are to be hung in retaliation for some of their men who were maltreated in some [way]. This is negro news, so we cannot vouch for it.

News has also been brought in by a "reliable" contraband that Mr. and Mrs. Hal Noland had been robbed of their money and the rings taken from Mrs. Noland's fingers, that the Yanks went to Mrs. Batchelor's and robbed the man who has leased her place and is staying there of $1,000. He said he would have killed them all if the women had allowed them. We cannot know how true this is, so we posted William off to hear the particulars. It is almost time for his return. I am inclined to believe it as some wretches went to Col. Cook's about a week ago at night to rob him. His sister, Mrs. Brabston, was quite badly choked in attempting to defend him.

We can have no relief for these wrongs, as Gen. McArthur told a lady the other day who went to him for a guard or protection paper against their trepidations. "No we came here to plunder and we will do it." This same general is in command during McPherson's absence, for he together with Sherman is off on a raid, their object we think being Mobile.

We have heard that our men are making a stand at Meridian.[28] We have also cut off the Yankees' provision train, and the Yankees acknowledge that our men are between here and Sherman's forces. We have Generals Polk and Lee[29] and others in command.

There were a set of thieves from the Bridge last Sunday in pursuit of plank,[30] but Mrs. Batchelor begged that they would not destroy any more of her houses. The Major consented for his men to go somewhere else, although the wagon master said they had better take what they wanted and burn the rest. It is evident that we are not to be allowed a day's rest.

MONDAY, FEBRUARY 15, 1864

The report we heard yesterday of the robbery has proved but too true. William returned late in the evening bringing all the news. Saturday night after Mr. and Mrs. Hal Noland had retired, someone knocked at their bedroom door.

Mr. Noland called out, "Is that you, Alonzo?"[31] (a negro)

"Yes, and you had better open that door."

Mr. Noland put on some clothing, but the door was burst open, and a pistol put to his head with the demand for his money. He told his wife to give it to them. The amount was about $200. They took her wedding ring off her finger, also a diamond one, all her jewelry and even her velvet cloak. The latter they took out on the gallery and left. Mrs. Joe Noland wrote me a note from Mrs. Batchelor's giving me an idea of what they had undergone at that place.

Dear Miss Emily,

You may think we have seen sights during the siege and since, but the scene we passed through last night beggars all description, but we will try to give you a few of the principle events. I was sitting upstairs in my room reading; it was just ten o'clock, and Sister Ellen had just got in bed and was asleep, of course. We heard some one come up to the front door, but I thought it was Mr. Birney.[32] The first thing I knew was Jennie rushed upstairs to me and said, "Aunt Vic, the robbers are downstairs and have threatened to kill Ma if she don't open the door." Of course I was terrified and wanted to know if she had waked Mr. Birney up. She said yes, and the first thing I knew he was upstairs leaning over the front bannister and wanting to shoot the men, but he said he thought they were Confederates, and I then begged him not to shoot, for I did not then know they had threatened Sister Ellen. The men then broke the door open and rushed in Miss Mary's room and asked her where her money was, at the same time pointing a pistol in her face. They then ran upstairs after Mr. Birney, took his pistols away from him, and made him give up his pocket book. They then got around him and pointed pistols at his head and breast. Sister Ellen and I begged and implored them not to kill him, that he was a Northern man, and one of them said he had "orders to shoot everyone who had arms." They then slipped around to Mr. Birney's room, getting his watch and the balance of his money, which made in all $1,000. They kept on saying they wanted money and were going to have it. Their faces were all blacked up, but that did not keep us from recognizing the same men that came here a few days ago. Mr. Birney has gone to the bridge to see if he can do anything. Annie and Sister Ellen have gone also to try and get guards. They did not take anything from any of us but Sister Ellen's cameo pin. There was a good many things that happened that would take me too long to write. It was an hour of terror to all of us, for I never in the whole of my life have seen such looking wretches. Their pistols were drawn on us all of the time, but one of them said in an undertone to me, "Don't be frightened, keep quiet, and we will not hurt you." We all send love to Mrs. Downs and hope you may never experience the terror we endured last night. William will tell you all about Hal and Annie. They got such a nice haul at these places that they did not stop at Mrs. Bolls.

Your affectionate friend,
V.N.[33]

SUNDAY, FEB. 21, 1864

Nearly a week has elapsed since I last wrote. Monday it rained, but in the evening I walked over to Mrs. Batchelor's, found all looking as usual, though they had such a terrible fright. Mrs. Batchelor and Mrs. Noland went to the Bridge to get guards. Gen. Tuttle, who is in command there, refused to give them any, said he would do all he could to discover the robbers, etc.

Mrs. Batchelor said the men put pistols to her head and demanded her money. She said she had none.

"Where do you get anything to eat, then?"

"I draw rations," she said.

All the time she had her little money in her pocket. If they had ordered her to turn it inside out, as they did Mrs. Noland, they would have taken quiet possession of her little all.

Mrs. Booth and Annie were at Mrs. Batchelor's.

The negro cavalry were out after a negro deserter.

Tuesday and Wednesday I walked over to school. Thursday it snowed, Friday it was cold, and I felt far from well, concluded not to go.

Tuesday a man from Wisconsin was here to lease this place.³⁴ He came back yesterday while Mrs. Batchelor and Mrs. Noland were here. He said he was not able to be [here] all the time so brought out with him a young man to superintend the place in his absence.

After this man, Mr. Westcott, had gone out to look around, we heard the front door open and a man walked into the room dressed out in a full suit of Confederate uniform. We all looked at him in surprise, for he evidently was not a Yankee.

"Why," Mrs. Batchelor exclaimed, "You are not a Yankee."

"No indeed," he said.

"You are a western man," I then proposed.

"Yes," he said.

"Well, you are all Yankees to us," Mrs. Noland said, "as you are fighting us."

I said, "He is not a Yankee. Look at his feet," which were very small.

Someone said perhaps he was a deserter. He acknowledged that he was. We told him he ought to be ashamed to confess it and said he would never have confessed it had he been one, so we would not believe him. He said nevertheless he was a deserter, that he belonged to the 6ᵗʰ Texas Cavalry, that his horse died. He was unable to buy another and his command refused to give him another but transferred him to the infantry. He says he would not be in the infantry service, so deserted.

Mrs. Batchelor told him if she had known it she would have slipped him a horse from here. We told him he should have stolen a horse from some citizen there. He said he could not steal, but we told him it was better than deserting. All the time I could not help feeling sorry for the poor fellow. It must have been the clothes he wore which excited our sympathies.

SUNDAY, MARCH 5, 1864

We are having the most delightful weather in the world. I never saw more delightful weather as we have had this winter with the exception of the freezing time about the 1ˢᵗ of January.

The Yankees are around and as busy as ever. Gen. Sherman came in last week with his staff. This week McPherson and all the army are coming in. Yesterday about 800 contrabands³⁵ were brought in. They were taken immediately to Vicksburg, these men put into the army and the women and children either left to starve or put on board transports and carried to some plantation to be hired. Poor negro – their freedom did not last long. Their destiny is to make cotton, although some declared they would never pick a bale of cotton again.

We hear numberless reports of the success of the Yanks on their trip to Mobile, or whatever they went for. We at least feel certain that they did not succeed as they did not get beyond Meridian. Gen. Polk was ready for them there.

Some of the Yankees were here yesterday who went out on the expedition. They say in their return they passed through Canton and burnt it up, also Livingston.[36] I would not be surprised. But we can rely on nothing we hear. Some say they passed through Canton rapidly, as Lee's Cavalry[37] was close on them. Mrs. Batchelor asked some of them if some of their number had not gone "on to Richmond." They acknowledged the fact.

A negro man from Mrs. Batchelor's on his way from town yesterday picked up a little negro boy about four years old. He says his mammy lost him. She had a barrel of meat and had no room for him in the wagon and pushed him out. He said he belonged to Mr. Wiggins of Livingston. Some Yankees told us yesterday that negro women were actually wrapping their children in cotton and burning them up to get rid of them. This is a terrible fact. The poor negro is a great sufferer by this war.

Vic and Pattie came in about two weeks ago. They had had a fine time in the Confederacy.

Last Wednesday morning Mr. and Mrs. Noland left for Louisiana. We were all very sorry to see them go. They have been with us 18 months nearly.

I am still with Mrs. Downs, walk back over to Mrs. Batchelor's in the morning and return in the evening.

I received a letter from Alice Vaughn. Mr. Moore is anxious for me to come teach for him. I feel tempted to go at times, but cannot make up my mind to leave kind friends here.[38]

SUNDAY, MARCH 14, 1864

Mrs. Booth got in from Dixie a few days ago. She says Sherman's retreat was a complete defeat. Our soldiers are very jubilant and indeed they have cause to be as success crowns our sons on every side. Banks was whipped at Madisonville by Dick Taylor[39] and pushed back to New Orleans perfectly furious. Forrest[40] whipped Grierson (the famous Yankee raider who thought he could go through Mississippi when he pleased, as he succeeded once), who consequently failed to meet Sherman. It was said Sherman was loud in his praises of Gen. Stephen Lee and his cavalry. He says he could whip the world with such a general. Gen. Lee had sent him word that he had whipped him twice before and would do it again. The Yankee Cavalry were so demoralized that they were obliged to bring out their infantry to fight our cavalry. Gen. Polk has made himself a name – our good Bishop of Louisiana.

Gen. Sherman made his headquarters at a gentleman's house in Clinton. This gentleman's daughter, a young lady, did not appear at the supper table, and before a crowd of Yankee officers Gen. Sherman ordered her to be sent for. She came and took her seat.

"You do not choose to eat with Federal officers, I presume."

She spiritedly replied, "You can oblige me to sit at the table with you, but you cannot force me to eat."

When they returned to the parlor he ordered her to the piano and obliged her to play about two hours. The next day on their leaving he went to her and said, "When I next see you I hope you will have a thick-lipped negro for your husband."[41]

The old dog. She ought to have told him that would suit his own daughters better, if he has any. That is the way with them. When they cannot whip our men they take their spite out on our poor women and children.

Our success in Florida has been glorious. Even the Yankee papers admit a defeat and are anxious for something to be done with Seymour[42] who was in command. Gen. Thomas has been obliged to fall back from Tunnel Hill.[43]

Last week Mrs. Batchelor went into her parlor one night and who would be sitting on one of her chairs but a big black negro, hail fellow well met, with those Yankee Lessees. She ordered him out in a few moments, told him he knew better than to [be] seated in her parlor. He retreated and the next day apologized, said the Yankees made him sit down. She told him not to sit down in her house again. The men looked very silly.

Last Monday the first thing she knew a wagon came out with trunks, and towards night here drove up a buggy with one of her Lessees, Mr. Ditridge, his wife and two children. Mrs. Batchelor never noticed them [but] allowed him to take her into his room. When tea was ready she sent them word. They came around, no one said a word. Mr. Ditridge went to Mrs. Batchelor and said he would like to get board for his family. She told him no, she could not get along as it was. So the next morning they started off before breakfast. The impertinence. After taking everything and forcing people' own negroes into the army to fight against them, turn around and ask favors. No. Southern hospitality towards the North should cease.

FRIDAY, MARCH 18, 1864

Last Monday Vic Batchelor and I went to Vicksburg. We had already heard previously that a young friend of Vic's from Sharon, Madison County, had been taken prisoner in the late raid, so our first visit was to the jail to ascertain the truth. We went to the guard and inquired for Divine,[44] a Confederate prisoner. The guard called out, "Divine, a rebel prisoner." One fellow sitting outside said, "A Confederate, you fool you." Mr. Divine was not long in making his appearance. He was delighted to see Vic. When she told him that she was going to try to get him out on parole of honor, his face became radiant.

We left him and went to Gen. McPherson, who gave him a parole of ten days to report in that time. The General told us to go to his Provost Marshal across the street and present the release. We did so, and then waited two hours for Mr. Divine's appearance. The Provost Marshal said he had sent it to Col. Waddell, the provost marshal of the city. It was strange the prisoner was not brought around.

We at last concluded to go and see for ourselves. Went to the jail, there had been no release. We went to the Court House and found the Colonel writing, utterly unconscious of our hurry. We stated the case to him. He looked among his papers and there it was, ordered a guard, and in a few moments we were at the door, and Mr. Divine was released. He was the happiest fellow. His first words were, "Well, Miss Vic, I never will forget you for this." We conducted him to the Provost Marshal where he took his parole, and then we all got in the carriage and swung out home.

EPILOGUE

Emilie McKinley ended her diary abruptly and disappeared from the pages of Warren County history. Perhaps she accepted Mr. Moore's teaching job, wherever it was, which was mentioned in her diary.

About the time she quit writing, in the spring of 1864, many of the plantations along the Big Black River in Warren County were leased to Yankee speculators who hoped to make a quick fortune off cotton, which was selling for the unheard of price of a dollar a pound. The new breed of planter, called a lessee, was sometimes well intentioned but knew nothing of operating a plantation. Confederate guerrillas took delight in destroying any physical progress they made and relentlessly harassed the lessees with the intent of driving them out of the community.

Mrs. Batchelor leased Hoboken to three men who occupied a wing of her house, bought equipment, and built a corral for their horses and mules.

Across the river in "Rebeldom" were Confederate scouts under the command of Capt. W. A. Montgomery, who had been raised along the Big Black and knew the locations of every low-water crossing.

One night Montgomery and a dozen of his men headed toward the Batchelor plantation. They surprised a picket, who had gone to sleep at his post, and arrived at the house undetected. As the men surrounded the house, the captain stepped to the door and demanded that it be opened; the only answer was the click of the rifles from within. Montgomery stepped back a few paces on the gallery, then rushed toward the door, forcing it with his shoulder. It gave way, and, with a six-shooter in his hand, he sprang into the room, which was illuminated only by the dying embers in the fireplace. In the faint light he saw a man, pistol in hand, in what appeared to be an open door leading to another room.

"Surrender!" Montgomery demanded as he raised his pistol and drew down on the form in front of him. He heard someone running, but the man in the doorway seemed to defy him as he leveled his pistol at the captain without saying a word. As Montgomery pulled his trigger, the fire blazed, and he realized he had just shot his own image reflected in a full-length mirror on the door of an armoire beside the doorway.

A search revealed the hiding places of all three lessees under the beds and sofas. The Confederates took their guns and valuables and on the way out also took the mules and horses from the corral. The Yankees soon abandoned the idea of raising cotton and returned to the North, and Mrs. Batchelor leased the place to an Englishman, E. Cordwent, who quickly made friends with Captain Montgomery.[1]

In 1870 Congress established the Southern Claims Commission, which was to receive and evaluate charges against the federal government made by Southerners who stated that they had been loyal citizens during the war but had lost possessions to the Union army. Though some Southerners were pro-Union, many who were not filed claims anyway, hoping to recoup some of what they believed had been illegally taken from them by the Yankees.

Among the thousands who filed a claim was Ellen Batchelor, whose petition asking for reimbursement was made 4 September 1871. In addition to 51 bales of cotton she said were taken, other items had been procured or purloined in the months of May through August 1863 by troops commanded by Generals Osterhaus and Dennis. Mrs. Batchelor, who owned Hoboken but also had interests in the various Noland plantations, filed for all of them. She asked for reimbursement for 25,000 bushels of corn, 10 horses, 150 head of cattle, 50 mules, 500 hogs, 3,000 pounds of bacon, 300 sheep, 1,000 bushels of potatoes, and 3 wagons, totaling $47,550.[2]

According to the petition, Mrs. Batchelor claimed that she had been loyal to the government of the United States and had given no aid or comfort to the enemies thereof. The claim was denied, partially because the government stated she could not prove that she was the sole owner of the plantation where the losses occurred. The government also seriously doubted her loyalty. Concerning her loss of cotton, however, the court of claims ruled in her favor, awarding her $9,055.05 for 51 bales, paying her $177.55 a bale,[3] far less than the dollar a pound the stolen cotton probably brought some carpetbagger.

In later years Mrs. Batchelor again pursued the claim when a bill for her relief was introduced in Congress on 27 April 1888 and referred to the court of claims on 1 May 1888. The original claim, minus the cotton bales, was introduced, but on 26 August 1893 the case was dismissed "for want of prosecution."[4]

In 1890, when a reunion of the Blue and the Gray was held in Vicksburg, and thousands of old soldiers returned to the Confederate fortress, Mrs. Batchelor made a personal visit to meet the son of General Osterhaus. She told him the story of how his father had returned her silver, and she expressed her appreciation.[5] In later years the Batchelor home burned, and only one piece of the silver was saved.

Mrs. Batchelor's oldest son, Thomas, survived the war just three years, dying in 1868 when he was only thirty. He was buried in the plantation graveyard near his father. His brother George, who was an attorney, became a farmer after the war and also served in the state senate. In 1876 he married a neighbor, Jennie Aldridge. He died in 1908 and was buried at St. Alban's Episcopal Church. His sister Ellen, the youngest of the children, did not marry; she preceded her brother in death by a year and was buried at St. Alban's. What began as a business venture for Mrs. Batchelor ended in matrimony for her daughter Eugenia: she married E. Cordwent, the Englishman who leased the plantation, in 1887.

Victoria—"Miss Vic"—Batchelor married but did not change her name, for in 1875 she wed J. M. Batchelor, a cousin from Amite County, Miss. They made their home in Warren County, where they farmed and also raised a large family. Miss Vic, described by a neighbor as a woman of "vivacity and humor, which were striking characteristics of her nature,"[6] died 8 May 1904 and was buried at St. Alban's.

Mrs. Ellen Batchelor had been a widow for forty-three years when she died in December 1893, only a few months after her claim against the government was dismissed. She was buried beside her husband and near her parents and son at Sligo.

After the siege of Vicksburg, Miss Vic had expressed misgivings about whether or not Isom Marshall, one of the slaves, would remain loyal to the family and to the Confederacy. He had been in Vicksburg with Dr. Thomas Batchelor but then joined George Batchelor in Virginia for the rest of the war. In his old age Isom was given a pension for his Confederate service, but in 1912 the rolls were being purged of any who might not deserve the monthly allotment. When Isom's name came up for review by the pension board, Capt. W. A. Montgomery recalled that when the war ended, young George Batchelor wept copiously. Isom threw his arms around his master and consoled him, saying, "Don't cry, Marse George. You did the best you could, and you are not to blame."[7]

There was no question of Isom's loyalty, and his name remained on the pension roll for the rest of his life.

NOTES

PREFACE

1. Arthur E. Bostwick, *A Life with Men and Books*, 17.

2. Ibid. Also see *The War of the Rebellion: A Compilation of the Official Records of the Union and Confederate Armies*, 1st series, vol. 41, 137.

PROLOGUE

1. Lida Lord, "A Woman's Experiences," *Century Magazine* (April 1901), as quoted in A. A. Hoehling, *Vicksburg: 47 Days of Siege*, 19.

2. James L. Autry was the colonel commanding the post at Vicksburg. His correspondence concerning the demand by Farragut is in *The War of the Rebellion*, 1st naval series, vol. 18, 492–93.

3. Richard Wheeler, *The Siege of Vicksburg*, 158.

4. Mary Loughborough, *My Cave Life in Vicksburg*, 159.

5. Emma Balfour's diary, 17 May 1863.

6. Dora Richards Miller's diary. 17 May 1863.

CHAPTER 1: "MY BLOOD BOILS AS I WRITE"

1. Mrs. Noland was probably one of the sisters-in-law of Mrs. Batchelor.

2. Stephen S. and Ann Valentine Booth were neighbors and close friends of the Batchelor family. They had two sons in the Confederate army, Roswell and David Booth.

3. Fleming was a slave who belonged to Mrs. Batchelor.

4. Needham B. Lanier and his wife, Eliza, and five children lived on Baldwin's Ferry Road southeast of Vicksburg and not far from Mount Alban.

5. Mose was a slave who belonged to Mrs. Batchelor.

6. Mr. Short was an officer in the Union army.

7. Mary Downs was a widow who was Mrs. Batchelor's closest neighbor. The fifty-three-year-old woman's household included several of her Aldridge kin.

8. Annie was a horse.

9. Sligo Plantation had belonged to Mrs. Batchelor's father, Pearce Noland, and was located near the Big Black River. During the war it was the home of Henry Peyton "Hal" Noland and his wife, the former Annie Robinson Aldridge. Peyton served in Cowan's Battery, a Confederate unit from Warren County.

10. Thomas Vaughn Noland was one of Mrs. Batchelor's brothers. He was captain of the Warren Volunteers at the beginning of the Civil War but soon resigned and returned to Warren County because of poor health. He and his wife, the former Lydia Julia Tigner, had four children—Agnes, Amelia, Ellen, and Ada.

11. Anderson was a slave who belonged to Mrs. Batchelor.

12. Parker was a slave who belonged to Mrs. Batchelor.

13. Dr. David Booth was the twenty-one-year-old son of S. S. and Ann Booth and was a member of the Volunteer Southrons.

14. Baldwin's Ferry Road connected Vicksburg and Utica, a town some thirty miles to the southeast, and the ferry was a main crossing on the Big Black River.

15. "Marse Pearce" was Pearce Noland, Jr., one of Mrs. Batchelor's brothers. He had married Elizabeth McGaughey in Warren County on 20 May 1858.

16. Ned Booth was a slave who belonged to S. S. Booth.

17. Mrs. Folkes, the former Rebecca Newman, was the widow of Miles C. Folkes, who had been mayor of Vicksburg from 1840 to 1845. He died 27 August 1860 at age fifty-three.

18. Mrs. Alex Newman was Margaret McGaughey before her marriage to Alexander F. Newman, a planter near Bovina.

19. Mrs. Green, the former Eliza Newman, was the wife of Washington Green, a planter and former president of the Warren County Board of Police, which was the governing body of the county.

20. Dr. J. C. Newman, who married his cousin, Laura G. Newman, lived near Mount Alban. He died 15 September 1889 at age seventy-six, and his wife died on 6 October 1878 at age fifty-four, during the yellow fever epidemic. Both are buried in the old Mount Alban Methodist Church Cemetery.

21. Alex Newman was Dr. J. C. Newman's brother. One of their sisters, Lucinda, married Elon G. Marble, and another, Lucille, married A. Folkes. All lived in the Bovina community. Alex Newman, born in 1812, died in 1887; he spent several years in a mental institution.

22. John Alexander McClernand commanded the Thirteenth Corps in the Vicksburg campaign. Like Lincoln, he was born in Kentucky and grew up in Illinois. In Congress he was a moderate Democrat who attracted the attention of Lincoln, who needed to hold southern Illinois Democrats to the cause of the Union. Though McClernand had only a few months of military service (as a private during the Blackhawk War in 1832), the president gave him a commission as brigadier general of volunteers. A major general by 1862, McClernand sought to supplant Gen. George McClellan in the eastern theater and criticized Gen. U. S. Grant in the west. After a fatal assault upon the Confederate works at Vicksburg on 22 May 1863, he furnished the press with a congratulatory order, calling his men the heroes of the campaign. Grant removed him from command, but in 1864 he again commanded the Thirteenth Corps in Louisiana and Texas. He resigned from the army on 30 November 1864.

23. Ulysses Simpson Grant, an Ohio native who became the ranking general of the armies of the United States, was a West Point graduate and a veteran of the Mexican War. He resigned from the army on 31 July 1854 but was unsuccessful at most endeavors in civilian life. He began service during the Civil War as a colonel of the Twenty-first Illinois Infantry, though he had offered his services to the adjutant general in Washington and to Gen. George B. McClellan. Through the political influence of an Illinois congressman, Elihu B. Washburne, he received an appointment as brigadier general of volunteers, to rank from 17 May 1861. His reputation was

greatly enhanced with his victories at Fort Henry and Fort Donelson and then at Shiloh. Despite a severe setback in the fall of 1862, when Confederates captured and destroyed his supplies, Grant methodically began an attempt to take Vicksburg, concluding with the siege in 1863. It was his most brilliant victory, sealing the fate of the Confederacy.

24. Peter Joseph Osterhaus, a native of Germany, was one of the Union's most distinguished foreign-born generals. He received a military education in his native land but fled to the United States in 1849 after revolutions had swept Europe. He first lived in Illinois and then moved to St. Louis, entering federal service on 27 April 1861 as a major in a Missouri battalion. He fought at Elkhorn Tavern and Wilson's Creek and was named a brigadier general in June 1862. In the Vicksburg campaign he directed a division and was wounded at Big Black River. He eventually returned to Germany where he died 2 January 1917 at age ninety-four.

25. William Plummer Benton, a brigadier general in the Union army, commanded a brigade of the Thirteenth Corps, first under McClernand and then under Gen. Edward O. C. Ord. Though born in Maryland, he was reared in Indiana, where he was the first in his county to respond to Lincoln's call for volunteers in 1861. His previous military experience had been as a private in the Mexican War. In the Civil War he saw service in western Virginia and in Missouri before taking part in the Vicksburg campaign.

26. Rebecca Aldridge was probably a niece of Mrs. Downs and was about twenty-one years old in 1863. She married George Batchelor on 19 January 1876.

27. Amanda Brien, who was married to A. W. Brien, lived near the Big Black River a few miles east of the Batchelors.

28. Warren County citizens were justifiably proud that one of their own, Jefferson Davis, who lived south of Vicksburg at Brierfield Plantation, was chosen president of the Confederate States of America.

29. Lloyd Tilghman, a Confederate brigadier general who commanded the First Brigade of Gen. W. W. Loring's division in Gen. Earl Van Dorn's Army of the West, had been taken prisoner at the fall of Fort Donelson and held prisoner until the fall of 1862. At the battle of Champion's Hill in May 1863, he was directing artillery fire when he was struck in the chest by a piece of shrapnel and died instantly. The arrival of his body in Vicksburg, transported in a wagon and accompanied by his teenage son, was described by Vicksburg writer Maria I. Johnston in a novel in 1869: "Stark and stiff lay the brave officer, his clothing and gloves covered with blood, and the gory stream congealing in the dark masses of his tangled hair. . . . " Maria I. Johnston, *The Siege of Vicksburg*, 18–19. Tilghman was buried in the city cemetery, Cedar Hill, but his body was moved to New York City after the war.

30. The churchyard referred to was St. Alban's Episcopal, which the Batchelors attended.

31. Fort Warren, in Boston harbor, was used to house Confederate prisoners, including General Tilghman.

32. The Bowman House was the leading hotel in Jackson, the capital of Mississippi, fifty miles east of Vicksburg.

33. Border ruffians in Kansas, led by abolitionists such as Jim Lane, who became a United States senator from that state, were usually called Jayhawkers, the term sometimes being used for all Kansas troops.

34. Mr. Street was probably the overseer.

35. The younger Batchelor children were Ellen and Eugenia.

36. Mary and Sue were slaves who belonged to Mrs. Batchelor.

37. Gabe was a slave.

38. Harris was a slave.

39. Myra and Lucinda were slaves.

40. Mrs. E. B. Willis lived a few miles northeast of Vicksburg. Her home became headquarters for Gen. John A. Logan during the siege.

41. Mrs. Thomas Brabston was the former Ara Ann Newman and a neighbor of the Batchelors. She and her husband were married in 1839.

42. Mrs. John Brabston was the former Nancy C. Reese. When she and her husband married in 1850, she was eighteen, and he was thirty-two.

43. Mary Brabston was about twenty-one years old in 1863. The daughter of Mr. and Mrs. Thomas Brabston, she married Samuel Townsend, Jr. in 1865.

44. The Alex Cooks and their two children, Thomas and Mary D., lived near Mount Alban.

45. Kezziah was a slave who belonged to Mrs. Batchelor.

46. Jim was a slave.

47. Old Charles was a slave.

48. The two-mile bridge, so called because of its distance from Vicksburg, was a railroad trestle.

49. The home of James Ferguson was located on Baldwin's Ferry Road and near the four-mile bridge, another railroad trestle. The wounded occupied not only the house but also outbuildings and tents on the lawn. Grant had planned an attack on the city on 22 May at ten in the morning, but the Confederates repulsed the enemy, inflicting terrible casualties. The Union lost three thousand men, the South five hundred. Almost every large home near the fighting was converted to use as a hospital. Grant was convinced that a siege was the only way to take Vicksburg.

50. Alfred was a slave.

51. Yucatan was a plantation.

52. Miss Mary may have been a reference to Mary Brabston or to Mrs. Downs.

53. Jennie Aldridge resided in the Downs home.

54. Adm. David G. Farragut's fleet had shelled the city in 1862 in an unsuccessful attempt to take Vicksburg. The shelling in 1863 was from the guns on Adm. David D. Porter's vessels.

55. Andrew Bolls was a brother of Henry Bolls and was about fifteen years old at the time of the siege. He died in 1887.

56. George Thompson was a minister, originally from South Carolina, who pastored Mount Alban Methodist Church.

57. James Richard Slack, born in Pennsylvania, moved as a young man to Indiana, where he was an attorney and served in the state senate. He was commissioned a colonel of the Forty-seventh Indiana Infantry on 13 December 1861 and commanded a brigade under Gen. John Pope at New Madrid. He took part in the White River expedition and the engagement at Yazoo Pass. During the Vicksburg campaign he commanded a brigade of Hovey's division of McClernand's Thirteenth Corps.

58. Annie Boylen was a horse, possibly the same one referred to earlier as "Annie."

59. Thomas Gibson, who was in his mid-fifties and lived near the Laniers just off Baldwin's Ferry Road, was married to Minerva Kline; they had five children.

60. Eugene Asa Carr, a West Point graduate from New York, had a distinguished career in the army, serving much of the time on the frontier. In the Civil War he fought at Wilson's Creek and Elkhorn Tavern. Wounded three times at the

latter, he was given the Congressional Medal of Honor for distinguished gallantry. At Vicksburg he commanded a division of the Thirteenth Corps. The word of his death was a false rumor.

61. Frederick Steele, a West Point graduate from New York, served with distinction in the Mexican War. He entered the Civil War as colonel of the Eighth Iowa, advanced to brigadier general in January 1862, and took part in the Arkansas campaign that year. He commanded a division of Gen. W. T. Sherman's forces in the attack at Chickasaw Bayou north of Vicksburg in the winter of 1862, and during the campaign the next year directed a division of the Fifteenth Corps. The news of his death was also false.

62. Alvin Peterson Hovey commanded a division of the Thirteenth Corps at Vicksburg. An Indiana native, he was an officer of volunteers in the Mexican War but saw no military service. At the beginning of the Civil War he was commissioned colonel of the Twenty-fourth Indiana and saw service in Missouri and at Shiloh. In the Vicksburg campaign he was a division commander of the Thirteenth Corps. In December 1863 he was sent home on a military assignment.

63. Miss Priss was probably a sarcastic reference to one of the Newman girls, either Sallie or Louisa, daughters of Dr. J. C. Newman, and Chesley was a probable reference to his youngest daughter, Mary Chesley, who would have been about ten years old in 1863.

64. Mr. Phillipps is unidentified.

65. Gus Downs is unidentified.

66. Possibly J. T. Hicks.

67. Mrs. Young was probably Mrs. Hal Young, no relation to Captain Young, a Confederate soldier from Missouri.

68. There were at least five Union generals with the surname of Smith in the Vicksburg campaign. The identity of this one is undetermined.

69. Capt. Upton Miller Young, originally a member of Gen. Sterling Price's army, had transferred to Pemberton's army and was captured in one of the battles in the Vicksburg campaign that preceded the siege. Captain Young was paroled and confined to the area around Mount Alban. After the war he came back to Vicksburg, married, and was an attorney and judge before returning to Missouri in the 1880s.

70. Egypt was a plantation on the Big Black River.

71. Greenfield was one of the Noland plantations.

72. Vicksburg historian M. J. Mulvihill told a story of Union troops visiting Oakley, the Booth's plantation home, and one of them picking up a pan of milk to drink. As he lifted it to his lips, Mrs. Booth struck the bottom of the pan, splashing milk into his face and all over and exclaiming, "There, you pig!" Mulvihill, who was also Vicksburg postmaster in the 1920s, wrote the story and other accounts of the Booth family in 1935 after an inquiry to the Chamber of Commerce from W. H. Green of Belleville, Ill., concerning items found with the remains of a Michigan soldier whose skeleton had been unearthed years before on the Vicksburg battlefield. Included had been items with the Booth name on them, items that had no doubt been taken from the family home. Copies of Mulvihill's correspondence are owned by Mrs. Eric Biedenharn of Vicksburg. An account of the story was published in the *Vicksburg Sunday Post* on 9 October 1977.

73. Miss R. A. R. may have been Rebecca Robinson.

74. Joseph Eggleston Johnston, a Virginian and graduate of West Point, had been commander of Confederate forces in Virginia until he suffered a wound at Seven Pines; Pres. Jefferson Davis replaced him with Gen. Robert E. Lee. When

Johnston recovered, Davis placed him in command of the Department of the West. He was later instructed to assist Pemberton at Vicksburg, a job he kept planning but never undertook. During the siege, Johnston's army was headquartered in Madison County at Canton, northeast of Vicksburg and due north of Jackson. Johnston's reluctance to aid Pemberton could be blamed partially on his dislike for Davis, a feeling that was mutual.

75. Snyder's Bluff was located along the east bank of the Yazoo River north of Vicksburg and was part of the Battle of Chickasaw Bayou in late 1862.

76. Fred Grant was the twelve-year-old son of Gen. U. S. Grant who, at his father's suggestion, accompanied him to war. The general praised him for being "very manly." He was not a captain on his father's staff, but in later years he did graduate from West Point and pursued a military career. William S. McFeely, *Grant: A Biography*, 45, 81.

77. William Tecumseh Sherman was widely renowned among Union generals, second only to Grant in fame. A native of Ohio, he was a graduate of West Point. During the Mexican War he was breveted a captain for meritorious service in California. He resigned from the army in 1853 and became a banker, then moved to Kansas and practiced law, and then in 1859 became superintendent of a Louisiana college. He moved to St. Louis in 1861 and soon was a colonel in the Thirteenth U.S. Infantry. Sherman's star rose rapidly but not without controversy, as he had a volatile temper, was quick-spoken, and was often at odds with the press. His scorched earth policy while marching through Georgia and South Carolina earned him eternal hatred by many in the South. He discovered first-hand that many Southern women were unforgiving and bitter, an example being when he met a group of them at Parson Fox's home north of Bovina in the summer of 1863. He found it impossible and useless either to defend himself or argue and hurriedly vacated the scene. For a full account of the affair, see William T. Sherman, *Memoirs*, vol. 1, 329–30.

78. Ship Island, the location of Fort Massachusetts, was off the coast of Mississippi in the Gulf of Mexico, near Biloxi. After being captured by the Union it was used to house Confederate prisoners.

79. Mrs. Philip Phillips, whose husband was a congressman from Alabama before the war, was imprisoned in August 1861 in Washington, D.C., along with her two daughters and charged with being suspected of disloyalty. Once she was released she moved to New Orleans. In 1862, after the fall of the city, she was arrested for laughing during the funeral procession of a Union soldier and was accused of teaching her daughters to spit on Yankee officers. Taken before Gen. Benjamin F. Butler, she denied the charges and refused to apologize. He sentenced her to be confined at Ship Island and said she should be regarded and treated as "a common woman." See *The War of the Rebellion*, 2nd series, vol. 4, 105. Already hated by many Southerners, Butler earned the title of "Beast Butler" for his treatment of Mrs. Phillips. The diarist's reference to pieces of candle is unexplained.

80. The rumors of damage to the church were exaggerated, as McKinley states at a later date in her diary. However, before the war was over, the church was desecrated by Union soldiers before they completely demolished it. Church historian Marion B. Bragg wrote, "After the destruction of the church, Amelia Bigelow Barr went into the churchyard and picked up some broken glass from the windows. Sadly and sorrowfully she wrapped them up and carefully put them away 'for sentiment's sake.'" Marion B. Bragg, *St. Alban's Protestant Episcopal Church*, 10. The Bigelow

sisters—Sarah, Amelia, and Mary—were born in Canada. In Vicksburg the three ladies were milliners, and their brother, Wilson, was an architect. He joined Cowan's Battery in 1861, and his sisters moved from the city to the family plantation a few miles northeast of the Batchelor home.

81. E. and Margaret Evans lived a few miles from the Batchelors. She was born in Ireland, he in Wales, and their three children were born in Pennsylvania.

82. Elon G. Marble owned a plantation on Clear Creek near the Big Black River. His wife, the former Lucinda Newman, died several years before the war, and two of his sons were killed in Confederate service in Virginia. One Union soldier in August 1863 wrote of the beauty of the family cemetery and recorded the lengthy epitaph for Mrs. Marble. For a full account, see the diary of Sgt. Thomas K. Mitchell of the Fourth Illinois Cavalry, 15 September 1863. According to Mrs. Virginia Brabston Cook, historian of the Bovina community, in an interview with the editor on 30 June 1997, other Union soldiers later broke open the vault to rob the grave of jewelry the corpse was reportedly wearing; Mrs. Cook's ancestors, the Camerons, reburied the body. A similar story of grave-robbing by Union soldiers was told by Jennie Wilson Floweree in her memoirs, published in the *Vicksburg Evening Post*, 29–30 March 1935.

83. Cotton money was issued by the state on the planter's baled cotton and was of value until the Yankees came, when it was either destroyed or seized and sold by the invaders. Without state backing it was worthless. Richard A. McLemore, *A History of Mississippi*, vol. 1, 498.

84. Probably Mrs. Alexander Cook.

85. Charlotte Spears, a widow, owned a farm near the Big Black River bridge on the Warren County side.

86. Old Billy was a slave.

87. Jack Black was a slave.

88. Hinds County was the area directly across the Big Black River east of Vicksburg. The Yankees referred to Hinds as "Rebeldom."

89. Camp Chase was a prisoner of war camp in Columbus, Ohio.

90. John Stevens Bowen, born in Georgia, entered Confederate service in Missouri, where he had been an architect before he became a captain of Missouri militia. A West Point graduate, he advanced rapidly under Generals D. M. Frost, Leonidas Polk, and John C. Breckinridge. He was promoted to brigadier general, and, following distinguished service trying to stop Grant's advance at Port Gibson, he was promoted to major general. His health was undermined by dysentery during the siege, and he died only a few days after the surrender. He had known Grant in St. Louis, so during the preliminary surrender talks he was appointed by Pemberton to confer with the Union commander.

CHAPTER 2: "THEIR IMPERTINENCE IS UNPARALLELED"

1. David and Jane Gibson's son, Edward, was twelve years old in 1863.

2. Henry Bolls was the son of John Franklin and Susan Potter Bolls. He was born 6 December 1844 and died in 1882. He is buried in Mount Alban Methodist Cemetery.

3. Alice was a horse.

4. Bovina was a railroad village about eight miles east of Vicksburg and only a few miles from the Big Black River.

5. Land was acquired for the Bovina Masonic Lodge from A. B. and A. S. Cook on 10 February 1858. Among members of the lodge were some of the Nolands.

6. G. W. Powell, a Virginian, and his wife, Mary, from North Carolina, lived near Bovina. Their only son was Alexander. The other children were Carolina, Georgiana, Martha, Anna, Eliza, and Laura. Martha married a Union soldier from Missouri, Sylvester Montague Hasie, and they lived in Warren County after the war.

7. A "teister," or tester, similar to a canopy, is a framed cover above a bed that is supported by the bedposts.

8. Possibly William Cooper, a forty-six-year-old farmer from Tennessee who lived south of the Batchelors on the Big Black.

9. Probably Joseph Noland.

10. W. Webb was an overseer for the Nolands. At the time of the siege he was forty-three years old. His son, Will, may have been the G. W. Webb who was a member of the Swamp Rangers, a local Confederate unit.

11. Eliza was a slave.

12. Amite, in south Mississippi, was the home county of Napoleon B. Batchelor before he moved to Warren County.

13. Satartia was a village on the Yazoo River north of Vicksburg and in Yazoo County.

14. Mrs. Eveline McGaughey and her family were related to the Nolands by marriage, for on 20 May 1858, Pearce Noland, Jr. married Elizabeth McGaughey; she was eighteen, and he was thirty-three.

15. "Young Mr. Brick" could have been Dean, Charles, or John Jr., all sons of John Brick, a New Jersey–born bricklayer who lived in Vicksburg.

16. Johnnie McGaughey was about thirteen years old and was the son of J. H. and Eveline McGaughey.

17. Citizens, who were often destitute because their homes and farms were in the lines of march of the armies, applied to Union army camps for provisions in order to feed their families and their slaves. Three weeks after the surrender of Vicksburg, a commissary was established at Bovina so that local citizens would not have to go into Vicksburg for badly needed supplies.

18. James Birdseye McPherson made his headquarters in the home of Dr. and Mrs. William T. Balfour on Crawford Street, only four blocks from the courthouse. McPherson, from Ohio, was a West Point graduate who began his service in the Civil War as a first lieutenant and rapidly rose to major general. He served under Gen. Henry W. Halleck and then as chief engineer to U. S. Grant. In January 1863 he was named commander of the Seventeenth Corps in the Vicksburg campaign. Of all the Union generals, he was the best liked by local citizens because of his courtesy and compassion. He was killed on 22 July 1864 in Atlanta.

19. Milliken's Bend, La., about fifteen miles upriver from Vicksburg, was a depot for Union army supplies in the summer of 1863, guarded by a detachment of white soldiers and two African American units, many of them raw recruits. Confederate forces attacked on 7 June 1863. After fierce fighting, the Union forces won but suffered about eighty black casualties, proving that, contrary to popular opinion, black soldiers would stand and fight. Confederate commander of the Trans-Mississippi, Gen. Edmund Kirby Smith, was not at the battle. Martha M. Bigelow, "The Significance of Milliken's Bend in the Civil War," *Journal of Negro History* 15, no. 3 (July 1960): 156–63.

20. Martha Miller was a slave.

21. Catherine was a slave.

22. Port Hudson, La., twenty-five miles upriver from Baton Rouge, was manned by seventy-five hundred Confederates who resisted forty thousand Union troops in 1863 in the longest true siege in American history. Union forces attacked the Confederates on 26 May 1863, resulting in over two thousand casualties for the North, six hundred of whom were African Americans. Rumors that Port Hudson had fallen persisted, but the actual surrender did not occur until 9 July 1863. Richard N. Current, ed., *Encyclopedia of the Confederacy*, vol. 3, 1238–39.

23. Most black soldiers in the Union army were slaves who had run away or were taken from the plantations by the advancing troops, and after the Emancipation Proclamation on 1 January 1863, Lincoln called for four Negro regiments. Gen. Ben Butler had already organized the Louisiana Native Guard, called the Corps d'Afrique, on 27 September 1862, followed by two more regiments. All regiments were commanded by white officers. There was speculation that the all-black units would not be good soldiers, that they would not stand and fight, but the opposite was true. Mark Mayo Boatner III, *The Civil War Dictionary*, 584–85.

24. Dr. Daniel Burnett Nailer was a Warren County physician who lived in the Asbury community about ten miles from the Batchelors. Mrs. Nailer was the former Teresa Selser Martin.

25. Called the "ironclad oath," citizens were urged and sometimes required to take an oath of allegiance to the United States promising not to aid the Confederate cause in any manner. The oath was a bitter pill for most Southerners to swallow.

26. Jared Reese Cook, who owned several plantations including Hard Times between Bovina and Vicksburg, was a Unionist who received protection papers signed by General Grant. His wife, Minerva Hynes Cook, was murdered by Union soldiers on 3 April 1865, and several were hanged for the crime.

27. Johnnie was a slave.

28. Asa Hartz was the pen name of a Southern officer, Maj. George McKnight of Loring's staff, who was a prisoner at Johnson's Island, Ill. His writings were published in the Northern press and were extremely popular. McKinley's diary reference is unclear. Gordon Cotton, "Asa Hartz (Say It Aloud) Became Famous As a Poet in Prison," *Vicksburg Sunday Post*, 13 December 1998, sec. B, p. 1.

29. Letty remains unidentified.

30. As the Union officer considered himself a gentleman, he did not argue, reply, or defend himself when the women heaped verbal abuse upon him.

31. Mrs. Tigner was the mother of Mrs. Vaughn Noland, the former Lydia Julia Tigner.

32. Mrs. Lane was probably either Laura Lum Lane, married to Edward M. Lane, or Catherine Hamilton Lane, married to Newit Vick Lane. The two men were cousins.

33. Mrs. Rebecca Sexton, a widow, lived near Antioch Church on Fisher's Ferry Road southeast of Vicksburg.

34. Mrs. Frank Gibson is unidentified.

35. Mrs. Tully Gibson was the former Kate Folkes and was the second wife of Dr. Gibson, who served in Virginia with a Mississippi unit and was murdered by carpetbaggers in the Mississippi Delta in 1870. See the *Vicksburg Weekly Herald*, 15 January 1870, 5 February 1870.

36. Earl Van Dorn, who commanded the Confederate Cavalry under Gen. John C. Pemberton, was a native of Claiborne County, Miss., south of Vicksburg. He was a West Point graduate who saw service in the Mexican War and in the Indian

campaigns of the west. He entered the Confederate service as a colonel, rose to brigadier and then to major general. He fought at Elkhorn Tavern and Corinth, but his most noteworthy achievement was the destruction of Grant's supply depot at Holly Springs, Miss., in December 1862. Van Dorn was murdered at Spring Hill, Tenn., on 7 May 1863 by a jealous husband. It is doubtful that any blacks were in Van Dorn's cavalry, but there were African Americans in Confederate service; the numbers are disputed, as is the extent of their participation. Some free blacks purchased Confederate bonds and offered to fight for the South, and both free and slave carried guns and saw action in battle. Most served as teamsters, cooks, and manual laborers or were personal servants. The Confederate government made an attempt near the end of the war to arm black units, but it was too late to make a difference in the South's struggle for independence. The role of blacks in combat, though contrary to law, was verified by the Northern press. *Harper's Weekly* on 10 January 1863 ran a front page story and engraving, "Rebel Negro Pickets," and Thomas Knox of the *New York Herald* wrote of Confederate sharpshooters at Vicksburg who were black. Wheeler, *The Siege of Vicksburg*, 91. Southern states rewarded many blacks for their loyalty with small pensions.

37. George and Eliza Hawkins owned a farm near Mount Alban. He was a native of Missouri, she from Tennessee. In the 1870s he filed papers with the Southern Claims Commission for losses suffered during the war. He was a Unionist, and his claim was allowed.

38. Clement Laird Vallandigham, an Ohio Democrat who served in the U.S. Congress, was vehemently opposed to the policies of Abraham Lincoln. He was imprisoned by the Lincoln administration and then banished to the South.

39. Leonard Wood was an outspoken Southern sympathizer who lived in Fall River, N.Y. When he rejoiced at the news of the assassination of Lincoln, he was beaten and kicked, and a mob wrecked his store.

40. John Brown, an antislavery fanatic who murdered proslavery men in the Kansas Territory, later appeared in Maryland across the Potomac River from Harpers Ferry, Va. On the night of 16 October 1859, Brown and eighteen followers took possession of the armory, arsenal, and engine house at Harpers Ferry, planning to free slaves and start an insurrection. A detachment of marines, commanded by Col. Robert E. Lee, easily overpowered Brown and his men. Brown was tried for treason against the state of Virginia nine days after the attack and hanged on 2 December 1859.

41. Despite the spelling—Sumter—the Yankee soldier was no doubt referring to Sen. Charles Sumner of Massachusetts. In May 1856 Sumner delivered a lengthy address before the Senate, "The Crime against Kansas," which he declared was "the rape of a virgin territory, compelling it to the hateful embrace of slavery. . . . " He launched into personal attacks upon some of his colleagues, including Sen. Andrew P. Butler of South Carolina. His invective was so insulting that a young kinsman of Butler, Congressman Preston Brooks of South Carolina, determined to punish Sumner, choosing to beat him with a cane as one challenged only a social equal to a duel but chastised a dog with a stick. The beating took place in the Senate chamber when it was not in session. Sumner, beaten into unconsciousness, became a martyr and did not return to the Senate for three years. Some charged that it was a sham, but nevertheless, though he claimed he was physically unable to serve, the people of Massachusetts reelected him. It is an irony that his cousin, Sister Ignatious Sumner, a member of the Catholic Sisters of Mercy in Vicksburg, nursed wounded Confederate soldiers in Mississippi and Alabama.

42. Wood was a horse.

43. Mr. Johnson is unidentified.

44. Julia was the wife of Thomas Vaughn Noland.

45. "The Death of Ellsworth" was a Union song telling of the death of Ephraim Elmer Ellsworth, a soldier who was killed on 24 May 1861 while removing a Confederate flag from a building in Alexandria, Va.

46. Caroline was a slave who belonged to Mrs. Downs.

47. Julia was a slave who belonged to Mrs. Downs.

48. Henry Downs was probably a slave.

49. Bridgeport was a place on the Big Black River, north of Bovina, where some Confederates crossed into Warren County following the Battle of Big Black.

50. Albert Newman was the eleven-year-old son of Dr. Newman.

51. Miss Sally was probably Sarah Ann Newman, Albert's older sister.

52. Warren County residents often heard rumors that Johnston was coming to their relief; it was wishful thinking. No fighting of any magnitude is recorded as having taken place at Bridgeport on 24 June 1863, though two days earlier a battle had occurred at Hill's Plantation a few miles north, and skirmishes took place a few days later at Messinger's Ford. Edwin C. Bearss, *Decision in Mississippi*, 589.

53. Miss Arnold's name was Flora Ann.

54. Thomas B. Manlove was lieutenant colonel of Company G of the Forty-eighth Mississippi Infantry. He died in 1880 at age thirty-eight and is buried in Cedar Hill Cemetery in Vicksburg.

55. Rev. Mr. Gibson remains unidentified.

56. Joe was the husband of Mary; they were slaves.

57. Capt. George Barnes of Company I, Wirt Adams Cavalry, was married to Louisa Nailer. He is buried in Asbury Cemetery near Vicksburg.

58. Mrs. Barnes was the daughter of Jefferson and Eliza Gibson Nailer. Jefferson Nailer opposed Jefferson Davis for a seat in the state legislature in 1843. Davis lost; it was his entry into politics.

59. Raymond, the county seat of Hinds County, is located about thirty-five miles east of Vicksburg and is eighteen miles southwest of Jackson.

60. Brandon, the county seat of Rankin County, is located twenty miles east of Jackson.

61. John Cabell Breckinridge of Kentucky was a former vice president of the United States, having served under James Buchanan. He became a Confederate general and secretary of war. He commanded the Reserve Corps at Shiloh and in the summer of 1862 defended Vicksburg against Adm. David G. Farragut's attack. Though he lost an attempt to retake Baton Rouge, he distinguished himself at Murphreesboro, in Johnston's campaign to relieve Vicksburg, and at Chickamauga. Following the war he lived in England and Canada before returning to Kentucky.

62. Valuables, such as jewelry or coins, were concealed in socks and tied around the waist. The "contraband" she spoke of must have been a weapon used for defense, possibly a stick.

63. Possibly the diarist was speculating that if the South executed a prisoner, Young might suffer the same fate in retaliation. Though North and South had agreed on a prisoner exchange during the early stages of the war, problems arose from the start over the identification of legitimate prisoners. The breakdown of exchange was mired also in what to do with captured black Union soldiers. The Confederate government decreed that they should be turned over to authorities of state governments where they were captured, as they were considered slaves, and

white officers of black Union units were to be tried and executed. Both sides threatened executions in an "eye for an eye" scenario. The North ceased to participate in the exchange after July 1863, but in early 1864 Gen. Benjamin F. Butler was permitted to try another exchange. His talks with Confederate commissioner Robert Ould broke down when Ould agreed that blacks who had been free before the war would be treated as prisoners but refused to give the same status to those who had been slaves. *Encyclopedia of the Confederacy*, vol. 3, 1256–58.

64. Billy Miller has not been identified.

65. Thompson was the Methodist preacher at Mount Alban; McGarr has not been identified.

66. In late June 1863, Union troops tunneled beneath the fortifications of the Third Louisiana redan and set off explosives. Few were either killed or wounded, and the Confederates quickly sealed the breach. One African American within the Southern lines was literally blown to freedom, telling the Yankees when he landed that he thought he had been blown "about three miles." The man, whose name was Abraham, became the personal servant of Dr. Silas Thompson Trowbridge, chief surgeon of the Seventeenth Army Corps. In writing the account, Trowbridge stated, "Poor Abe was the dumbest mortal I ever saw." Silas Thompson Trowbridge, M.D., *Autobiography*, 144–49.

67. Sterling Price of Missouri, affectionately called "Old Pap" by his men, served in the Missouri legislature and as governor and also represented the state in Congress. During the Mexican War he was colonel of the Second Missouri Infantry and brigadier general of volunteers. He first opposed secession but accepted the command of the pro-Confederate Missouri Militia in May 1861. He was victorious against the Yankees at Wilson's Creek and at Lexington, Mo. He was later a major general in the Provisional Army of the Confederacy and served in Mississippi, Arkansas, and Texas. At the end of the war moved to Mexico, though he returned to Missouri the next year.

CHAPTER 3: "ENOUGH TO SICKEN THE HEART"

1. Joseph Hooker of Massachusetts graduated from West Point in 1837 and, though he was a mediocre student, demonstrated commendable qualities of leadership and ability. During the Mexican War he won the brevets of all the grades through lieutenant colonel for gallant and meritorious conduct. He left the service in 1853 but was unsuccessful at civilian life, so he sought a commission in the army. On 6 August 1862 he was given the rank of brigadier general. His ascent in the ranks is attributed to a mixture of ambition and friendships. Though he was successful in some ventures, he is best recalled as one of several generals chosen to lead the Union forces in an attempt to defeat Lee, which failed. In 1864, feeling that his abilities had been ignored, he asked to be relieved of command, a request to which Gen. William T. Sherman promptly obliged. He has the dubious distinction of having provided his name for women of questionable virtue who followed his army and frequented his headquarters.

2. As a point of honor, Pemberton insisted that his men would march out of their positions and stack arms. As their lines had not been broken during the forty-seven days of siege, he was determined that Union troops would not enter Confederate fortifications until after the surrender.

3. Col. John Aaron Rawlins, though born in Illinois, was of Southern ances-

try. An attorney and politician, he joined Union forces with a friend, U. S. Grant, and became his aide-de-camp. Grant considered him nearly indispensable, and as the general attained fame, Rawlins's star also rose with appropriate advances in grade until he was named brigadier general, the last such appointment made during the war. During the occupation of Vicksburg, Rawlins married Mary Hurlburt, a private tutor for the children of Samuel Lum, in whose home Grant made his headquarters. Hurlburt was a Northerner.

4. Mrs. Sophia Gildart Fox had a home in Vicksburg and also a plantation in the country. She was a sister-in-law of Parson Fox, the minister at St. Albans.

5. On the contrary, many of the men had grown weary and did complain. On 28 June, the forty-second day of the siege, an anonymous plea signed "Many Soldiers" was slipped into Pemberton's headquarters; it suggested his army might mutiny unless they received some relief. It has never been determined if the letter was from Confederate soldiers in Vicksburg or if it was psychological warfare planted by the enemy. A. A. Hoehling, *Vicksburg: 47 Days of Siege,* 240–42.

6. Lieutenant Martin is unidentified.

7. Though Young had been captured months earlier at the battle of Champion's Hill and released on a parole of honor, he was exchanged along with the officers taken prisoner at Vicksburg.

8. John Clifford Pemberton, commander of Confederate forces in Vicksburg, was a Pennsylvanian who cast his lot with the South because of personal convictions, though his Virginia-born wife no doubt influenced his decision. A West Point graduate, he had served in the Mexican War where he had known U. S. Grant. Pemberton was twice breveted for gallantry while serving under Gen. Zachary Taylor. In Confederate service, he commanded the Department of South Carolina, Georgia and Florida, rising in rank from brigadier to major general, and then to lieutenant general when he was assigned to the Department of Mississippi and Eastern Louisiana in 1862. Pemberton was hampered in his defense of Vicksburg by conflicting orders from Jefferson Davis and Joseph E. Johnston. Following his surrender and exchange he sought to prove his Southern loyalty and zeal by taking a reduction in rank and fighting until the end of the war. After several years in Virginia he returned to Pennsylvania, where he died 13 July 1881. Pemberton, often slow to act, never won the confidence of his men, and some mistrusted him because of his Northern birth, though he always had the complete trust of President Davis. Lee scholar and biographer Douglas Southall Freeman called him "one of the great men of the Southern Confederacy . . . a gallant and gifted man who paid as great a price for his devotion as circumstances exacted of an American." Freeman wrote that Pemberton was a "technically proficient soldier, in his theories of artillery was well ahead of most of his contemporaries." John C. Pemberton III, *Pemberton, Defender of Vicksburg,* vii, 4, 5.

9. Pemberton furloughed his men to go home for several weeks and to then reassemble at parole camps in either Enterprise, Miss., or Demopolis, Ala. Many were then sent as reinforcements to the Army of Tennessee and were in the Atlanta campaign.

10. Chickasaw Bayou, a few miles north of Vicksburg, had been the scene of a decisive Confederate victory in late December 1862, when Sherman's army was defeated in an attempt to take Vicksburg. During the siege in 1863 the site was in Union hands and was a landing for supplies.

11. Dr. Coffee is unidentified.

12. Capt. William Larkin Faulk of Company B, Thirty-eighth Mississippi Infantry, wrote in his diary on 9 July 1863 that none of the Negroes was allowed to pass through the lines with the other Confederate troops, and Col. William Pitt Chambers, another Mississippian who served at Vicksburg, told of attempting to get black Confederates past the Yankee lines. A year later Gen. U. S. Grant insisted on equal treatment for black Union troops. A copy of Captain Faulk's diary is on file at the Old Court House Museum in Vicksburg, Miss. Also see William Pitt Chambers, *Blood and Sacrifice,* ed. Richard A. Baumgartner (Huntington, W.Va.: Blue Acorn Press, 1994), 90, and *Encyclopedia of the Confederacy,* vol. 3, 1258. Grant did not acknowledge that there were blacks in the Confederate army.

13. Isom Marshall was a slave who belonged to Mrs. Batchelor.

14. Although John Dunlap Stevenson was born in Virginia, educated in South Carolina and worked as an attorney in Missouri, he sided with the North in 1861 and became a colonel of the Seventh Missouri (U.S.). During the battle of Corinth he headed a brigade under Gen. James B. McPherson and was promoted to brigadier general during the spring of 1863. During the Vicksburg campaign his brigade was in Logan's division of the Seventeenth Corps.

15. Carter Littlepage Stevenson, a Virginian, West Point graduate and veteran of the Mexican War, served under Gens. Pierre G. T. Beauregard and Edmund Kirby Smith in the Confederacy before commanding a division as major general in the Vicksburg campaign under Pemberton.

16. Jeremiah Cutler Sullivan of Indiana saw action in Virginia as a colonel of the Sixth and Thirteenth Indiana before being commissioned a brigadier general. He was later assigned to Rosecrans's Army of the Mississippi, was inspector general on Grant's staff and was then chief of staff for McPherson. His military experience before the Civil War had been in the Navy. After the war, he seldom practiced law, though he was a lawyer, but worked in minor clerical jobs.

17. Martin Edwin Green, who organized and commanded a cavalry unit of Missouri troops under Gen. Sterling Price, served as a brigadier general under Gen. John S. Bowen in the Vicksburg campaign. He was shot and killed by a Yankee sharpshooter on 27 June 1863.

18. Cheney and Amanda were slaves belonging to Mrs. Downs.

19. Ellen was a slave.

20. Fort Sumter in Charleston harbor, where the war began, was an important symbol for the South. The Confederates held it until near the end of the conflict.

21. There were five Union generals with the surname of Smith in the Vicksburg campaign; this one's individual identity has not been determined.

22. The Manlove home was on the corner of South and Cherry Streets, only a block from McPherson's headquarters.

23. Woodville, in Wilkinson County, was about 110 miles south of Vicksburg on the Mississippi-Louisiana border. It was the childhood home of Jefferson Davis.

24. Susan Virginia Cameron and her husband, Dr. Granville Cameron, lived near Bovina. In 1860 she was thirty and he was forty-one. They had three daughters—Florence, Minnie, and Effie.

25. Elias Smith Dennis of New York served as commander in Logan's division of McPherson's Seventeenth Corps in the Vicksburg campaign and was sent to the abandoned or leased plantations near Milliken's Bend across the river from Vicksburg in Madison Parish. After the war he returned to the area, married a widow, became a planter, and was elected sheriff of Madison Parish, La.

26. Louise was a slave.

27. Deer Creek is a stream that meanders through much of the Mississippi Delta above Vicksburg. Part of it was navigable in the 1800s.

28. Other than that he was a paroled Confederate soldier, Lieutenant Holmes has not been identified.

29. The man's actions indicated his respect for the private property of Southerners, something one would not expect from a Northern soldier.

30. Records for J. Q. Arnold, city sexton and proprietor of the city's first funeral home, show that a casket was bought on 12 August 1863 for a Mrs. Tigner who resided in the county "out on Big Black." The name appears as Ligner in some printed records. The Arnold ledgers are owned by the Old Court House Museum in Vicksburg, Miss.

31. Among those wishing to rejoin the Union was the state's chief justice of the supreme court, William Lewis Sharkey, who lived in Warren County, his plantation being near Jefferson Davis's place, Brierfield. Sharkey was later appointed provisional governor by Pres. Andrew Johnson.

CHAPTER 4: "THEY SHIVER AT THEIR OWN SHADOWS"

1. Rebecca Robinson may have been related to Mrs. James Brabston, who was a Robinson before her marriage. Lieutenant Holmes stayed at the Brabston home, Linden.

2. Willie Aldridge was a nephew of Mrs. Mary Downs; he was about ten years old.

3. William Wirt Adams, who saw service in the War for Texas Independence, was a Mississippi planter, banker, and legislator who recruited the First Mississippi Cavalry. For his service in the Vicksburg campaign, he was promoted to brigadier general.

4. I. J. Wolfe was a member of Wirt Adams's cavalry.

5. Col. Thomas Clement Fletcher, an early supporter of Abraham Lincoln, had been wounded in action at Chickasaw Bayou north of Vicksburg. He was colonel of the Thirtieth Missouri (U.S.) in the Vicksburg campaign and served as governor of Missouri, 1865–1869.

6. Ida was a slave.

7. Carroll was a slave.

8. Greenbrier was a plantation, probably one of several owned by the Nolands.

9. Gen. Sterling Price attacked federal forces at Helena, Ark., on 4 July 1863 but was repulsed and withdrew toward the south central part of the state.

10. The fight McKinley reported that took place on Halls Ferry probably occurred on Fishers Ferry, a parallel road south of Vicksburg. Capt. Isaac Robinson Whitaker and his scouts ambushed and killed a number of Union soldiers near the old Fennimore farm. The number of casualties had been greatly exaggerated in the rumor McKinley heard. The story has been told many times in the community where it occurred and was the subject of an oral history interview on 27 October 1953 with Mrs. Mary B. Hullum, conducted by Mrs. Eva W. Davis, who was director of the Old Court House Museum in Vicksburg. Charles Faulk penned a story about the episode for the *Vicksburg Evening Post* on 16 November 1952 after interviewing a member of the Whitaker family. The story was also related in *The Memoirs of James M. Gibson Jr.*, which was privately published by his descendants in 1961.

Mentions of Whitaker and his men are found in *The War of the Rebellion*, 1st series, vol. 32, pt. 2, 181–82, 227.

11. Hannah was a slave.

12. Mrs. Montgomery was probably the mother of Capt. W. A. Montgomery, a guerrilla leader from Hinds County.

13. On 13 September 1863, the Union gunboat *Rattler* was moored at the town of Rodney, Miss., in Jefferson County when twenty-two crewmen, including the commander, left the boat to attend worship services at the Presbyterian church. Confederate guerrillas were advised of the situation; they surrounded the building, and Lt. Cicero Allen demanded that the Yankees surrender. Someone fired a gun, which caused pandemonium as worshipers screamed and scrambled beneath pews for safety. A few Union sailors escaped, one by hiding beneath the hoop skirt of an elderly lady. No one was injured, but sixteen prisoners were taken. The *Rattler* was not captured, but it almost fell into Confederate hands at a later date. During the skirmish in the church, the boat turned its guns on the structure, one shell lodging in the front wall over a window. The story was told in detail by the late Marion B. Bragg in an unpublished manuscript, "The Battle of the Hymnbooks," which is in the files at the Old Court House Museum. Other accounts can be found in *The War of the Rebellion*, 1st naval series, vol. 26, 402–13, 438–51, 768–69; also, 1st series, vol. 61, pt. 4, 264; also, *Confederate Veteran Magazine* (June 1907): 281–82.

14. Martha "Pattie" Booth was the seventeen-year-old daughter of S. S. and Ann Booth.

15. Palmer and Bowers were Union soldiers.

16. Captain House is unidentified.

17. Charles Robert Woods began his war service as commander of the troops sent on the *Star of the West* to relieve Fort Sumter in Charleston harbor. He was colonel of the Seventy-sixth Ohio, served under Sherman at Chickasaw Bayou, and directed a brigade of Sherman's Fifteenth Corps in the Vicksburg campaign.

18. Colonel Williamson is unidentified.

19. Dr. Joyceline was a Union army physician. He and his wife lived at Linden, the James M. Brabston plantation, in the months following the fall of Vicksburg.

20. The Shermans lost one child to illness while the general was stationed in Mississippi. Willie Sherman, who was nine years old, became ill as the family left Vicksburg for Memphis near the end of September 1863. Dr. Roler, physician for the Fifty-fifth Illinois, was aboard the same steamboat; he diagnosed symptoms of typhoid fever and feared for Willie's life. At Memphis the child was taken to the Gayoso Hotel; medicine was procured and additional physicians were summoned, but Willie died the next day, 3 October 1863. Sherman wrote that Willie "thought he was a sergeant in the Thirteenth. I have seen his eye brighten, his heart beat, as he beheld the battalion under arms . . . he had the enthusiasm, the pure love of truth, honor and love of country, which should animate all soldiers." Sherman blamed himself for having brought his family to what he considered such an unhealthy climate. William T. Sherman, *Memoirs*, vol. 1, 344–49.

21. Possibly Robert Moss, who lived in Hinds County.

22. William S. Rosecrans graduated fifth in his class at West Point, served an uneventful ten years in the Engineer Corps, took no part in the Mexican War, and resigned from the army in 1854. His civilian pursuits were also unsuccessful. After the firing on Fort Sumter he became an aid to Gen. George McClellan. He was moderately successful in Virginia, but his defeat in Tennessee at Chickamauga spelled the end of his military career.

23. Braxton Bragg, a West Pointer with a gallant record in the Mexican War, was a planter in Louisiana when the Civil War began. He saw action at Shiloh and later led an abortive invasion of Kentucky. He was victorious at Chickamauga but was forced by Union troops to withdraw into Georgia, where he yielded command at his own request to Joseph E. Johnston.

24. The Rossmans were related by marriage to the Selser family and thus to the Newmans and many others. They lived near Warrenton, south of Vicksburg.

25. James Murray Mason, a former senator from Virginia, was a Confederate diplomat who, along with John Slidell, was forcibly taken from the British ship *Trent* by United States forces in the early days of the war, causing an international incident that almost brought England into the conflict on the side of the Confederacy.

26. Jacobinson is unidentified.

27. The *City of Madison* exploded and burned at the Vicksburg waterfront on 18 August 1863, killing 156 men, and the *Robert Campbell, Jr.,* loaded with supplies for Union soldiers at Vicksburg, burned mysteriously at Milliken's Bend, La., on 28 September 1863, with the loss of twenty-two men. Over sixty steamboats sank on the Mississippi, most in the St. Louis area. Some were no doubt accidents, as witnessed by Pvt. James Warren, an Illinois soldier who saw the burning of the *City of Madison*. The letter from Warren to his brother, dated 20 August 1863, is owned by Mr. and Mrs. D. D. Leffler of Newton, Ill.; a copy is in the files of the Old Court House Museum in Vicksburg, Miss. See also *The War of the Rebellion*, 1st series, vol. 48, pt. 2, 194–97.

28. The revenge McKinley feared had been going on for some time. On 25 May 1863, Brig. Gen. Alfred W. Ellet reported to Secretary of War Edwin Stanton that two of his ships had been fired upon on the Mississippi River by a band of Confederates about six miles above the town of Austin, Miss. Ellet returned the next day and landed his force, engaged the enemy, and then "burned the town of Austin, having first searched every building." Austin was located in north Mississippi, south of Memphis. *The War of the Rebellion*, 1st series, vol. 24, pt. 2, 431.

29. William was a slave.

30. Noland was probably referring to a type of material. Confederates, especially those from the west, often wore uniforms of jeans wool and cotton, while Union uniforms were usually of much finer material, such as jersey wool or broadcloth.

CHAPTER 5: "THE IRON HEEL OF DESPOTISM"

1. Joseph Anthony Mower was born in Vermont, raised in Massachusetts, and joined the Union army in Missouri. He entered the army in the Mexican War as a private; seven years later he was named second lieutenant of the First U.S. Infantry. In the Civil War he had an outstanding record as regimental, brigade, divisional, and corps commander, and he rose from colonel to brigadier general to major general. In the Vicksburg campaign, Mower directed a brigade of Sherman's Fifteenth Corps.

2. James Madison Tuttle, born in Ohio, began his Civil War career as lieutenant colonel of the Second Iowa. He saw service at Shiloh, and in the Vicksburg campaign he commanded a division of Sherman's Fifteenth Corps. He returned to Iowa in 1863 and ran for governor.

3. Logan's Scouts were probably under the command of Col. John W. Logan of Company C, Third Regiment of Cavalry of the Confederacy.

4. Brownsville was a village in northern Hinds County.

5. Clinton was a town several miles west of Jackson in Hinds County.

6. Canton was the seat of Madison County, and Sharon was a village several miles northeast of Canton.

7. Ida is unidentified.

8. William Wing Loring, a major general, commanded a division that became separated from the rest of Pemberton's army at the Battle of Champion's Hill. He was a Florida legislator and attorney before entering the army in the Mexican War, where he won the brevets of major and lieutenant colonel. In the Confederate army he served in Virginia, with the Army of Mississippi, and the Army of Tennessee. He was the senior major general on active duty when the war ended.

9. Abraham Buford, a Kentuckian who was a West Point graduate and veteran of the Mexican War, took part in the Vicksburg campaign and was later a commander in Forrest's cavalry.

10. Winfield Scott Featherston of Holly Springs, Miss., was a veteran of the Creek Indian War and served in the Mississippi legislature. He commanded a brigade in Loring's division in the Vicksburg campaign.

11. Sis was obviously one of McKinley's sisters. Joe has not been identified; perhaps he was a brother, or maybe Sis's husband.

12. Just the opposite was true. George Henry Thomas, who earned the nickname "Rock of Chickamauga," drove Bragg's army from its position at Missionary Ridge on 25 November 1863. A Virginian who fought for the North, Thomas was never again acknowledged by his sisters.

13. Mr. Nichols and Mr. Washington are unidentified.

14. Col. James Peckham was in the Twenty-ninth Missouri (U.S.), which was in Sherman's Fifteenth Corps.

15. This was an obvious mistake, as the name was Noland, not Nugent.

16. James Angel Fox, a native of Connecticut, had been in Mississippi since 1819 and was the senior member of the Episcopal clergy in the state in 1860. He was a planter, owning a plantation north of the Batchelors's. He was also rector of St. Alban's Church at Bovina.

17. Gen. John McArthur, a native of Scotland, was commander of the Chicago Highland Guards, a militia unit, before the war and entered the Union army as colonel of the Twelfth Illinois. He directed one of McPherson's Seventeenth Corps divisions during the Vicksburg campaign and was commander of the city following the surrender.

18. Though McPherson had won laurels in every battle in which he had participated, when Grant nominated him for a promotion there were some in the North who accused McPherson of being unduly sympathetic to Southerners. The young general's retort was that he had "done nothing to justify the suspicions of rebel sympathy, save what the dictates of humanity suggest. When the time comes that in order to be a soldier a man has to overlook the claims of humanity, then I do not want to be a soldier." Elizabeth J. Whaley, *Forgotten Hero*, 135.

19. Henry Stuart Foote, who represented Tennessee in the Confederate congress, was a former governor of Mississippi who also served in the U.S. Senate in the 1850s. He was a bitter and vocal opponent of Jefferson Davis.

20. Mrs. Dameron was a resident of Bolton, a town between Edwards and Clinton.

21. Samuel Townsend owned Owl Roost Plantation on the Big Black River south of the railroad bridge. The family was so pro-Union that John Townsend testified that he cut several fingers from his hand in order to keep from being con-

scripted into the Confederate army. He gave the testimony when he filed papers with the Southern Claims Commission after the war.

22. Henry Ward Beecher, a Congregationalist preacher who pastored in New England, was a rabid abolitionist who also advocated suffrage for women. Mark Mayo Boatner III, *The Civil War Dictionary*, 56. Beecher's congregation supplied rifles, called "Beecher's Bibles," for abolitionists in Kansas before the war.

23. Mrs. David (Jane) Gibson and her family lived several miles south of the Batchelors near Asbury Church, where Mr. Gibson was a planter.

24. Manning Ferguson Force entered the service as major of the Twentieth Ohio Volunteer Infantry. His military service was entirely under Gen. U. S. Grant and Gen. W. T. Sherman. In the Vicksburg campaign he commanded a brigade in McPherson's Seventeenth Corps and was promoted to brigadier general.

25. Mrs. Arnold has not been identified, though, from the comments by the diarist, she was probably associated with the abolitionist movement.

26. Nurse Hale was probably a reference to John Parker Hale, a senator from New Hampshire who was the first antislavery man elected, serving from 4 March 1847 to 3 March 1853. He was elected again in 1855 and served until 3 March 1865. He was impatient with the slow pace of the Lincoln administration when it came to freedom for the slaves. *Biographical Directory of the American Congress, 1774–1927*, 1045.

27. Benjamin Franklin Butler, a Democrat before the war, had supported Jefferson Davis for president in 1860; he later became a radical Republican. While military governor of New Orleans in 1862, he issued an order that Southern women who openly expressed their Confederate views should be treated as women of the street. He was accused of stealing silver from the home he used as headquarters. Davis declared him an outlaw, and Southerners dubbed him "Beast Butler." An account of Butler's support of Davis in 1860 can be found in Bruce Catton, *The Coming Fury*, 39.

28. Sherman, with twenty-five thousand men, left Vicksburg on 3 February 1864 with the intention of destroying the railroads in central Mississippi and also capturing Meridian, a city near the Alabama border. Opposing him were Polk's two infantry divisions under Gen. W. W. Loring and Gen. Samuel French, along with Gen. Stephen D. Lee's cavalry. Gen. Sooy Smith was to advance from Memphis to aid Sherman, but his forces were humiliated in defeat by Gen. Nathan Bedford Forrest's cavalry at West Point. The expedition lasted until 5 March.

29. Leonidas Polk, who was a West Point graduate, was also Episcopal bishop of Louisiana and was called "The Fighting Bishop." Stephen Dill Lee was the youngest lieutenant general in the Confederate army; he was appointed in 1864 when he was thirty. During the siege he was in charge of artillery. After the surrender of the city he was placed in command of the cavalry in the Department of Mississippi, Alabama, West Tennessee, and East Louisiana.

30. Union soldiers often tore down plantation buildings, taking the lumber, or planks, to build barracks for occupation troops.

31. Alonzo was a slave.

32. Birney was a Yankee who leased the Batchelor plantation.

33. Victoria Noland was the wife of Mrs. Batchelor's brother, Joseph Noland. They owned a plantation in Madison Parish, La., but spent the time during the siege with Mrs. Batchelor, as they were cut off from their home.

34. With no slaves and no capital, some Southerners leased their plantations to Northern investors, called lessees.

35. Slaves were termed "contrabands" by Gen. Benjamin F. Butler in the early

days of the war in an effort to circumvent the law and not return runaways to their owners. Butler explained to the secretary of war that he treated "the able-bodied negroes, fit to work in the trenches, as property, liable to be used in aid of rebellion, and so contraband of war." Butler reasoned that as Southern states had declared themselves out of the Union, the return of fugitive slaves was no longer applicable. Northern newspapers made the term "contraband" popular. Wayne Andrews, ed., *The Concise Dictionary of American History,* 249.

36. Neither Canton nor Livingston, which was twelve miles north of Canton, was burned.

37. The cavalry was commanded by Gen. Stephen D. Lee.

38. Alice Vaughn and Mr. Moore are unidentified.

39. There was a skirmish at Madisonville, La., on 11 February 1864 between Gen. Richard Taylor of the Confederacy and Union Gen. Nathaniel Banks. This skirmish preceded the second Red River campaign, which Banks undertook in the spring of 1864. Taylor was the son of Pres. Zachary Taylor and brother-in-law of Pres. Jefferson Davis.

40. Gen. Nathan Bedford Forrest was a notable Confederate cavalry leader in the war, and Col. Benjamin Henry Grierson, who was later promoted to general, conducted a raid through the state during the Vicksburg campaign. Despite the rumors, Forrest and Grierson were not engaged with one another in battle. Grierson's raid had been made to divert Pemberton's attention from Grant's movements.

41. Rumors such as this strengthened the home front's opposition to the Yankees.

42. Truman Seymour of Vermont, a West Point graduate who fought against the Seminoles in Florida, returned to that state during the Civil War, leading a Union army expedition in 1864. He was defeated at Olustee, the only major engagement in that state.

43. It was a false rumor, for the Confederates were driven from Tunnel Hill, Ga., in late February 1864 by troops commanded by Gen. George H. Thomas.

44. John Divine was a private in Company C of the Eighteenth Mississippi Regiment, which was organized at Canton, Miss., on 20 April 1861.

EPILOGUE

1. Horace S. Fulkerson, *A Civilian's Recollections of the War between the States,* 178–81.

2. Southern Claims Commission papers, *Ellen D. Batchelor v. United States,* commission no. 7143, report no. 10, 1880.

3. Charles G. Nott and Archibald Hopkins, *Cases Decided in the Court of Claims at the December Term, 1875, and the Decisions of the Supreme Court in the Appealed Cases,* 480–81.

4. Southern Claims Commission papers, *Ellen D. Batchelor v. United States,* in the Court of Claims, congressional no. 4364, December term 1892 and 26 August 1893.

5. The story has been told in the Batchelor family from generation to generation.

6. Roswell Valentine Booth, "Private Memoranda" (typescript by Mary Lois Ragland, 1995, from the original journal). Booth was writing a tribute to Victoria Batchelor at the time of her death.

7. Ibid.

BIBLIOGRAPHY

PRIMARY SOURCES

Diaries

Balfour, Emma Harrison. Mississippi Department of Archives and History, Jackson, Miss.

Faulk, Capt. Wiliam Larkin. Typescript in the Old Court House Museum, Vicksburg, Miss. The original was lost by Faulk descendants.

Miller, Dora Richards. Typescript in the Old Court House Museum, Vicksburg, Miss. The original is in the Special Collections of Tulane University Library, New Orleans, La.

Mitchell, Thomas K. Typescript in the Old Court House Museum, Vicksburg, Miss. The original is in possession of Harry J. Mitchell, Topeka, Kans.

Interviews

Cook, Virginia Brabston. Interview by author. Vicksburg, Miss., 30 June 1997.

Hullum, Mary B. Interview by Mrs. Eva W. Davis. Vicksburg, Miss., 27 October 1953.

Letters

Mulvihill, M.J. Letter to W. H. Green, 1935, Eric Biedenharn, Vicksburg, Miss.

Warren, Pvt. James. Letter to P. W. Warren, 20 August 1863, Mr. and Mrs. D. D. Leffler, Newton, Ill.

Journals, Magazines, and Newspapers

Century Magazine (April 1901)

Confederate Veteran Magazine (June 1907)

Harper's Weekly (10 January 1863)

Journal of Negro History (July 1960)

Missouri Historical Society Bulletin (January 1962)

Vicksburg Evening Post (16 November 1952)

Vicksburg Weekly Herald (15 January 1870, 5 February 1870)

Private Records

Arnold, J. Q. Funeral home records. Old Court House Museum, Vicksburg, Miss.

Booth, Roswell Valentine. "Private Memoranda." 15 September 1878–1 January

1915. Originally owned by Mrs. Eric Biedenharn, Vicksburg, Miss. Typescript in the Old Court House Museum, Vicksburg, Miss.

Bragg, Marion B. "The Battle of the Hymnbooks." Typescript, Old Court House Museum, Vicksburg, Miss.

Confederate pension applications of black citizens of Warren County, Miss. Old Court Museum, Vicksburg, Miss.

Genealogical research files for the following families: Batchelor, Bolls, Booth, Brabston, Cook, Downs, Folkes, Newman, and Noland. Old Court House Museum, Vicksburg, Miss.

Public Records

Marriage records for Claiborne, Jefferson, Warren, and Wilkinson Counties, Miss., and Madison Parish, La. Copies in the Old Court House Museum, Vicksburg, Miss.

Southern Claims Commission. *Ellen D. Batchelor v. United States.* Commission no. 7143, office no. 129, report no. 10, 1880, Civil Reference Branch (NNRC), National Archives. Congressional no. 4364, December term 1892 and 26 August 1893, U.S. Court of Claims, Washington, D.C.

Southern Claims Commission. *John Townsend Estate v. United States.* Commission no. 4220, report no. 4, 1874. National Reference Branch (NNRC); National Archives, Washington, D.C.

U.S. Census returns, 1850 and 1860, for Madison Parish, La., and Warren County, Miss. Copies in the Old Court House Museum, Vicksburg, Miss.

SECONDARY SOURCES

Books

Baumgartner, Richard A., ed. *Blood and Sacrifice.* Huntington, W.Va.: Blue Acorn Press, 1994.

Bearss, Edwin C. *Decision in Mississippi.* Little Rock: Pioneer Press, 1962.

Bolls, James. *Warren County Went to War.* Vicksburg: A Ralph Mason Publication, 1990.

Bostwick, Arthur E. *A Life with Men and Books.* New York: The H. W. Wilson Co., 1939.

Bragg, Marion B. *St. Alban's Protestant Episcopal Church.* Vicksburg: Hamer Memorial Library, 1963.

Brieger, James F. *Hometown Mississippi.* Privately printed, 1980.

Brooks, Marlene Rutland. *Warren County, Mississippi, Cemeteries.* Vicksburg: Privately printed, 1999.

Carter, Linda Gene Felter, ed. *The Journal of Wilkinson County History.* Vol. 2. Woodville, Miss.: The Woodville Civic Club, 1991.

Catton, Bruce. *The Coming Fury.* New York: Simon & Schuster, Inc., Pocket Cardinal edition, 1967.

Cotton, Gordon A. *Asbury: A History.* Vicksburg: Privately printed, 1995.

Current, Richard N., ed. *Encyclopedia of the Confederacy.* New York: Simon & Schuster, 1993.

Fulkerson, H. S. *A Civilian's Recollections of the War between the States.* Baton Rouge: Otto Claitor, 1939.

Gibson, James M. Jr. *Memoirs.* Privately printed, 1961.

Hoehling, A. A. *Vicksburg: 47 Days of Siege*. Englewood, N.J.: Prentice-Hall, Inc., 1969.

Howell, H. Grady Jr. *For Dixie Land I'll Take My Stand!* Vol. 1. Madison, Miss.: Chickasaw Bayou Press, 1998.

Johnston, Maria I. *The Siege of Vicksburg*. Boston: Pratt Brothers, 1869.

Loughborough, Mary. *My Cave Life in Vicksburg*. New York: D. Appleton and Co., 1864.

McFeely, William S. *Grant: A Biography*. New York: W. W. Norton and Co., 1981.

McLemore, Richard A., ed. *A History of Mississippi*. Vol. 1. Hattiesburg: University and College Press of Mississippi, 1973.

Pemberton, John C. III. *Pemberton, Defender of Vicksburg*. Chapel Hill: University of North Carolina Press, 1942.

Rowland, Dunbar. *Military History of Mississippi, 1803–1898*. Spartanburg, S.C.: The Reprint Co., 1978.

Sherman, William T. *Memoirs*. Vol. 1. New York: D. Appleton and Co., 1875.

Trowbridge, Silas Thompson. *Autobiography*. Vera Cruz, Mexico: Privately printed, 1872. Published under the direction of Elihu Root, secretary of war, with Brig. Gen. Fred C. Ainsworth and Joseph W. Kirkley.

Whaley, Elizabeth J. *Forgotten Hero*. Fremont, Ohio: Lesher Printers, Inc., 1966.

Wheeler, Richard. *The Siege of Vicksburg*. New York: Thomas Y. Crowell Co., 1978.

Reference Books

Andrews, Wayne, ed. *The Concise Dictionary of American History*. New York: Charles Scribner's Sons, 1962.

Biographical and Historical Memoirs of Mississippi. Vol. 1. Chicago: The Goodspeed Co., 1891.

Biographical Directory of the American Congress, 1774–1927. Ansel Wold, compiler. Washington, D.C.: U.S. Government Printing Office, 1928.

Boatner, Mark Mayo III. *The Civil War Dictionary*. New York: David McKay Co., Inc., 1959.

Nott, Charles G., and Hopkins, Archibald. *Cases Decided in the Court of Claims at the December Term, 1875, and the Decisions of the Supreme Court in the Appealed Cases*. Washington, D.C.: U.S. Government Printing Office, 1877.

The War of the Rebellion: A Compilation of the Official Records of the Union and Confederate Armies. Washington, D.C.: U.S. Government Printing Office, 1901.

Warner, Ezra J. *Generals in Blue*. Baton Rouge: Louisiana State University Press, 1959.

———. *Generals in Gray*. Baton Rouge: Louisiana State University Press, 1959.

———, and W. Buck Yearns. *Biographical Register of the Confederate Congress*. Baton Rouge: Louisiana State University Press, 1964.

———. *Biographical Register of the Confederate Congress*. Baton Rouge: Louisiana State University Press, 1975.

INDEX